"Foster and Hicks conduct workshops internationally in the development of interpersonal skills. For this book, they interviewed happy people from all walks of life, from the United States to Eastern Europe. The resulting personal stories, writing exercises, and quotes together inform and instruct the reader in the nine principles discovered by the authors in their travels. Recommended."

—*Library Journal*

"My plan was to read the book long enough to decide whether I would write a testimonial. In a short time I found myself in the middle of a remarkable torrent of brilliant ideas, all delivered in a warm and sturdy format. I realized that at some unnoticed moment I had changed, and was now reading because I was convinced the book would be of great personal value to me—it could help me find more happiness. It is a delightful and boundlessly valuable book, especially for those readers willing to explore the possibility that happiness is something we can all choose."

—Will Schutz, Ph. D.,
author of *Joy, Joy: 20 Years Later* and *The Human Element.*

How We Choose To Be Happy

The 9 Choices of Extremely Happy People—Their Secrets, Their Stories

How We Choose to Be

Happy

Rick Foster and
Greg Hicks

A Perigee Book

A Perigee Book

A division of Penguin Group (USA) Inc.
375 Hudson Street
New York, New York 10014

G. P. Putnam's Sons edition: April 1999
First Perigee edition: February 2000
Revised Perigee trade paperback: June 2004

Published simultaneously in Canada.

Visit our website www.penguin.com

Library of Congress Cataloging-in-Publication Data

Foster, Rick.
How we choose to be happy : the 9 choices of extremely happy people : their
secrets, their stories / Rick Foster and Greg Hicks.
p.   cm.
ISBN 978-0-399-52990-0 (alk. paper)
1. Happiness. 2. Happiness—Case studies. I. Hicks, Greg.
II. Title.
BF575.H27F67   1999   98-37033 CIP
                 158.1—dc21

Printed in the United States of America

10 9

For our children

Tim and Molly Hicks

Alex and Kathryn Foster

Acknowledgments

Our happiness journey has run through two eras—first, the research and writing of this book, and next, the amazing developments after its initial publication. From the beginning, it has been graced by so many who have championed it. Thanks to our editor and trusted friend, John Duff, at Penguin who nurtured and supported our work every step of the way, and to our agent Angela Miller. Thanks also for the skill and superb judgment of our independent editors: Marilyn Foster for her careful reading and insightful suggestions and Paula Munier for her knowledgeable and optimistic cheerleading through the writing process.

Ron Luyet, always gentle of spirit and compassionate about our human strengths and foibles, gave generously of his professional understandings and his materials, including the "List of Defenses." Thanks also to landscape architect Laurie Grassman of Boulder, Colorado, for her invaluable help with flora, to Dr. David Spear for his deep insight into the interaction of behavior and biochemistry, to Philip Turner and Tonda Marton for advice about writing projects in general, and to Tonda for giving us a "writer's retreat" in New York City.

Our first Happiness Workshops were sponsored by Dr. Barbara Scott in San Luis Obispo, California. Eva Nemeth transformed her physical therapy offices in Marina Del Rey, California, into a conference center on our behalf. A wonderful crew from Shelburne Farms, Vermont, including Emily Morrow, Alec Webb, Megan Camp and Paul and Eileen Growald, supported our work in their community. Thanks to all of them for adding to the demographic depth of the interviews and to our understanding of happiness.

We also have an extraordinary support system of friends and family who gave unconditionally to the early days of the project. Special thanks goes to dear friends—Ellen Tussman, Diane Jarmolow, Russell Kaltschmidt, Herb Kindler, Marilyn Ginsburg and Janet Cobb. Their referrals to interview sources, opinions and reactions were critical to the development of our ideas. Our generous and patient readers were our parents, Lenore and Don Hicks and Harold and Diana Foster. Matt Weinstein and Geneen Roth gave us a much-needed kick-start in the beginning. And "The Men's Group" continues to provide a superb forum to experiment, try out ideas, and receive loving yet firm feedback.

We also want to express our gratitude to Ailish and the late Will Schutz, who over the years taught us so much, and introduced us to the wonderful acupuncturist, Dr. Van Vu. His work kept us balanced, and gave us the energy to do our research, write a book, raise our children and continue working.

Since the initial publication of *How We Choose to Be Happy*, a great number of people and institutions have introduced us to professional arenas we couldn't have previously imagined. Our deepest gratitude goes to Duffy Newman and Joanna Infantine of the Health Forum in San Francisco, who gave us a superb entrée to the medical world. There is no way to individually thank all the wonderful people with whom we're partnering in the medical fields, but special thanks go to Doctors Nicholas LaRusso and Jeanne Huddleston of The Mayo Clinic, who astonish us with their drive for excellence. At Memorial Sloan-Kettering Cancer Center, Dr. David Jaques and Aileen Killen provided us with a life-altering view of surgery. Elizabeth Duthie, Director of Nursing for Patient Care Systems at NYU Hospitals Center, has been full of ideas and information and is an encouraging friend. And, Jenny Kirksey, Community Health Director of Wake Forest Baptist Hospitals has been a great supporter. We thank all of you who have become friends and colleagues.

Other faculty and organizational work has also been a source of inspiration and growth. Many thanks to Dr. Joseph Mori and Julie Ryan who have included us as faculty in their MSA program at San Jose State University. Becky Miles-Polka and Gail Hardinger have also given us faculty positions with the wonderful Iowa Community Health Leadership Institute. And James Baraz and Edith Politis have brought us into the unexpected delights of the Buddhist community at Spirit Rock Meditation Center in Marin County, California. You have all enriched our lives immeasurably.

Above all, we deeply thank the hundreds of "extremely happy people" from around the world, whose love, commitment, words and thoughts appear in these pages. There is no way to express fully our respect and gratitude to them. They have changed our lives, and we thank them deeply for the kindness, honesty and thoughtfulness they shared with us. Although their names and hometowns have been changed, their true spirits soar through every part of this book and continue to inform our lives.

A Note to the Reader

All of the names and locations of people in this book have been changed for reasons of confidentiality. In some instances, we also created composite interviews from narratives that were similar. But in all cases, the stories faithfully reflect the ideas and attitudes of the people we met and the accounts of their life experiences and philosophies.

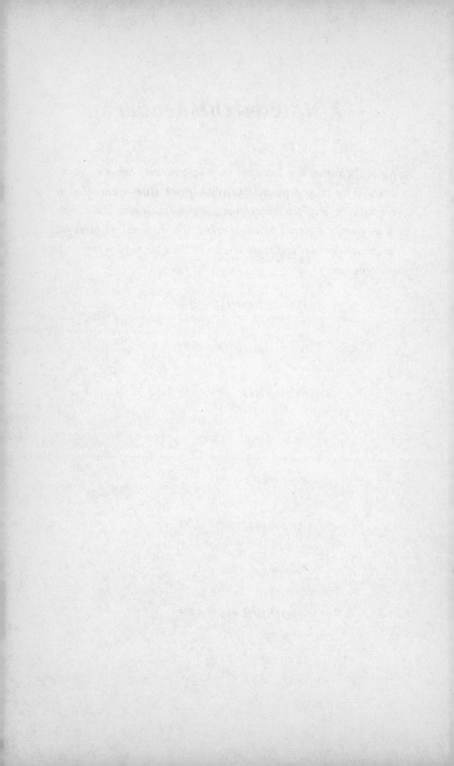

Contents

The universe is made of stories, not of atoms.

—Muriel Rukeyser

Prologue

The universe is made of stories, not of atoms.

—Muriel Rukeyser

Kathryn's Story—Part One

In one of my earliest memories, I am a beautiful ballerina flying through the sky in my pink tutu. I feel lighter than air. My leotard clings to me like a warm cocoon.

I am eight years old, in love with myself, in love with ballet, and very happy. I would not feel that kind of joy for another twenty-five years.

My childhood happiness ended with the realization of a legacy that doomed me. The legacy was my grandmother Kathryn—my namesake who died the year before I was born.

She was the mold my parents used to raise me. "Grandma K wouldn't have wasted her time dancing! Grandma K studied her lessons! You can't become a successful businesswoman like Grandma K if you don't get A's in math!"

If Grandma Kathryn had lived, I'm sure she would have liked me. I was a creative, beautiful little girl. But her ghost was a memory I couldn't escape. My parents had a picture of who I should be even though it had nothing to do with who I really was. Grandma K had been a great success at business. I was an artist.

By the time I was a teenager my real self had been buried. I had completely forgotten the little ballerina who loved flying through the air. I had become a different Kathryn. I was studious, serious, business-minded. I had set my course. I wanted to become an accountant and have a business like Grandma K's.

With my plan in place, I was determined to execute it. In the six months after college graduation in the late 1960s, I married my high school sweetheart, took a job as an actuary, and set up housekeeping. My parents were delighted. "Grandma K would have been so proud." I felt proud, too. I thought I knew exactly what I wanted and how life would turn out.

But something was wrong. I had lost the real me. And that creative but neglected and angry little girl came back to haunt me with a vengeance.

My demons were rumbling inside. Within a year I scandalized my parents. I quit my job and left my husband. It was the first divorce in the family and no one—and I mean no one—had ever walked away from a well-paid job. Everyone was so disappointed in me. All I knew was that I felt empty. I needed to fill myself up—with what, I didn't know.

Looking all the way back to 1971, I find it almost impossible to believe that the person in my story is really me! After quitting I spent six months hitchhiking with a friend from my home in Los Angeles to Florida. We went through the Sun Belt and deep into Mexico. The day after we arrived in Miami, my friend decided she was homesick and went back to California. Here I was in an unfamiliar city, with no job, no money, and didn't know a soul. I felt terribly sorry for myself. I was directionless and blamed the world for my situation.

Over the next three years I went through the worst period in my life. I had stopped caring about myself. I worked as a cocktail waitress in a seedy bar. I became bulimic. I had a series of abortions and finally ended up in the hospital with a tubal pregnancy. I was crying a lot of the time, completely unable to figure out why all this was happening to me.

One night I hit rock bottom. I accepted $1,000 to have sex with some guy I met at the bar. I did not know the man; but worse, I didn't know myself. Who was this person I had become?

That night I was overcome with such sadness and shame. Up until then I had justified my behavior by saying that the world had been harsh. My parents had been cruel—of course I had to starve myself! Of course I had to be a failure, how else could I take a stand against Grandma K?

But hitting bottom jolted me. I couldn't believe what had happened to my life. Looking back, this was the definitive moment when I began my long journey toward happiness. . . .

(To be continued in Chapter 2)

How We Choose to Be Happy

A Revolution in Happiness

In the ten years since we began our research, the study of happiness has changed radically. But nothing could have prepared us for the explosive growth in our own work. Updating *How We Choose to Be Happy* gives us a wonderful opportunity to reflect upon and share that amazing journey.

Back in the mid 1990's, we could never have imagined that a few conversations in a coffee shop in Northern California would lead us to a three-year voyage of in-depth interviews with extraordinary people from the back roads of Mississippi to the boulevards of Budapest. It was inconceivable to us when this book first came out in 1999, that our happiness model of nine choices would be used all over the world by universities, corporations, hospitals, and churches. And now, that same model has brought us to the halls of major research institutions, including the Mayo Clinic, NYU Hospital, and Wake Forest University Medical Center, where it's seen as a groundbreaking analysis of how people create happiness and a key to the mind/body connection.

This model has led us in other unexpected directions as well. From it, we've developed a template of ideal leadership attributes, currently used by some of the largest companies in the world. We now use it as a behavioral guide in shifting the cultures of organizations to profitability and high morale, as the focal point for team training, and as a behavioral interviewing instrument for hiring the best employees. It's also the basis for Greg's new book on how to be a Thriving Leader in these turbulent times, *LeaderShock And How to Triumph over It!* (McGraw-Hill). In non-business settings, it has been embraced as a strategy for relationships—among parents and children, teachers, social workers and therapists. And to medical people it's fast becoming accepted as a paradigm of behaviors that lead to better health and healing.

In short, we now know that this particular confluence of nine choices not only generates happiness for individuals, it also contains fundamental building blocks from which any healthy human grouping is made—families, teams, organizations, even entire communities. And from the standpoint of wellness, doctors are telling us that if you examine a human being at the cellular level, the same set of behaviors pumps-up biochemistry and encourages optimal health.

However surprised and honored we've been by these developments, our greatest delight is watching the model of nine choices transform lives. We now know that by following this system, people grow and change and, yes, *learn* to make themselves happier. This is what the book is about: helping you make choices that lead to greater happiness. We hope that this updated version of *How We Choose to Be Happy* will be an important addition to your life.

The Dovetail: Our Happiness Model and Scientific Research

What the Scientists Say

For most of human existence, happiness has been a non-measurable, self-reported emotional state. Where it comes from and what effect it has on our minds and bodies has been a subject of broad philosophical and academic speculation. But in the last decade, there has been a true revolution. With the availability of sophisticated technologies to measure the specifics of our blood chemistry, brain function, and genetic make-up, a remarkable canon of scientific studies on the mind/body connection has been completed. Previously undiscovered bio-immunologic markers have been found in our saliva and blood, and brain scans can mark even the most subtle changes in our neurological responses. But, though we know a great deal about the connection of emotions and physiology, how much do we really know about happiness?

The Happiness Controversy

The most widely quoted "hard" research of the past ten years has been by geneticists who tell us that we're each born with a happiness set point. Much like the "metabolic set point" that predetermines our natural body weight, our happiness set point determines our levels of cheerfulness and seriousness, called SWB or subjective well-being. Geneticists tell us that, regardless of what happens to us—whether it's an exciting financial gain or the tragic death of a spouse—we will eventually return to our set point. And, other than *extreme* poverty or disease, things such as age, race, income, and educational and family background seem to have almost no effect on how happy we'll be throughout our lives. In short, geneticists conclude that we have very little control over our own happiness.

On the other hand, behavioral researchers have found that we *can* do certain things to change the way we feel. For instance, they've discovered that exercise, diet, and meditation, along with other endeavors can cause beneficial changes in our brain function and biochemistry. They've also looked at depression, stress, anxiety, and trauma to see how our bodies respond to these emotions. By understanding the specific chemicals that are associated with certain feelings, they've documented what we've all observed—that our bodies under stress will be more disease-prone and less effective than when we're happy.

In spite of these revolutionary developments in the research world, the results appear contradictory. The biochemists say that there's much we can do for ourselves—making good choices will lead to healthy bodies and elevated levels of "happy" chemicals. The geneticists tell us that there is little we can do to change what we are hard-wired to feel. Impressive data. Excellent research design. So who's right?

Where We Weigh In On the Debate

Both sides of the argument are right. In years of studying hundreds of happy people, we discovered that they, indeed, started out with a myriad of set points. Some reported they were born cheerful, others reported being naturally pensive. But regardless of where they started, we consistently found that people who make the nine choices that we explore in this book, are able to elevate themselves dramatically *above* their starting point. While set points may be etched in stone, a large part of what generates happiness is cognitive. We have discovered that virtually everyone can learn to integrate these choices into their lives, regardless of their psychological makeup, family history, or other life circumstances. Unlike other happiness theories, these particular nine choices form an elegantly practical roadmap that prescribes exactly what to do. This unique blend of independent behaviors, when all are in full operation, come together to produce extreme happiness. And it is this discovery that has caught the attention of the medical world.

In fact, within the first month after publication of *How We Choose to Be Happy*, medical professionals began to step forward during our lectures and training programs. They told us we were studying far more than happiness. From years of their own professional observations, they concluded that our nine choices were the same ones being made by their most successful patients. This thinking took them to a provocative conclusion: The biochemistry of happy people is highly correlated to the biochemistry of healthy people.

We found this idea to be electrifying from the beginning, and immediately offered to partner in research.

To date, there is a diverse array of medical research in the works using our model. All of it seeks to affirm two major points: First, that happiness is a crucial determinant in health; and second, that less happy people can be trained to make themselves happier and, therefore, healthier.

Our research falls into five main areas: general healthfulness, healing, adherence to healthy courses of treatment (what the experts refer to as "compliance"), pain management, and finally, a multi-billion dollar field that affects us all—the relationship of happiness to submission of medical insurance claims. From immune response to speedy hospital discharge, we are correlating happiness with bodies that heal faster and respond better to medical treatment. We are looking at the relationship of repeated heart attacks and happiness, and measuring the happy individual's richer production of antibodies after a vaccination. And, we know from anecdotal observation that happy people are far more likely to follow a medical regimen carefully, and to make fewer unnecessary trips to the doctor.

Beyond the many social and economic implications of this work, each of these areas offers us all special insight into the enormous impact of the mind/body connection on health. And, as we train doctors, nurses and patients to use the happiness model in medical treatment, we will have new tools to improve health and respond more effectively to injury or disease.

Within the next few years the final results of these long-term quantitative studies will be published. Early returns are positive, and the qualitative experiences of medical people all over the world suggest that our work will be successful. Indeed, the mind/body connection is becoming clear and we are convinced that happiness and health are one.

The Definition of Happiness

Inherent in the discussion on happiness is a fundamental roadblock. In our modern world, happiness is ill-defined. Variously referred to as contentment, joy, pleasure, satisfaction, elation, cheerfulness, "sunny-ness," and ecstasy, there is no real "there there" on which to anchor our discussion.

In our own research, we went to the source and asked extremely happy people how *they* define happiness. What we heard was that true happiness is a profound, enduring feeling of contentment, capability, and centeredness—the 3 Cs. It's a rich sense of well-being that comes from knowing you can deal productively and creatively with all that life offers—both the good and the bad. It's knowing your internal self and responding to your real needs, rather than the demands of others. And it's a deep sense of engagement—living in the moment and enjoying life's bounty. This complex feeling is the direct result of the nine choices, all working together in a synergistic system.

The complexity of this definition is fascinating and provides some rationale as to why happiness has been so difficult to study. To happy people, happiness is multi-factoral. But what they've *not* included in the definition is absolutely stunning. While they report feelings like enjoyment and pleasure, to happy people, there is a dramatic distinction between the momentary positive feelings that money can buy, and the richer, longer term, more affecting emotion of true happiness.

Our Journey to the Happiness Model

At the beginning of this odyssey, we were corporate leadership consultants, traveling from one Fortune 500 Company to another, watching the mounting toll of stress, not only on the people with whom we worked, but on ourselves. We also noticed something else. There were a handful of unusual individuals who stood out from the crowd. They seemed to live in a different world from the rest of us. They had life "wired." Regardless of the problems swirling around them, they moved through life with a grace, warmth, and vigor that was both alluring and mysterious. There was only one way to describe them: extremely happy. And, we were fascinated by them.

So we shifted direction, deciding to focus our attention on the world of profoundly happy people, not just at work, but in every aspect of life. We had so many questions. What makes them tick? How do they stay emotionally elevated? What are they doing that the rest of us aren't?

We set out to discover the secrets of happy people. Instead of mailing surveys or conducting phone interviews, we chose to talk with people face to face. We wanted to see how they live, watch them interact, and get to know them on their own turf. So we hit the open road, stopping in both large cities and small farming towns—and everything in between—where we simply asked the locals, "Who's the happiest person around?" They'd caucus and proffer a name. We'd track down their suggested subject and invite ourselves over. To our amazement, people all over the world knew exactly what kind of happiness we were talking about; and never once were we turned down. Before this stage of our research ended, we'd sat in more than three hundred living rooms throughout the U.S. and Europe, feasting on and absorbing happy people's insights into the fundamental nature of happiness.

Our off-beat research methodology and the amazing people we met along the way were emotionally moving, invigorating and downright fun. We traveled to rural Alabama to talk with the fourth generation owner of a hardware store. We shared a meal with a cafeteria worker in the barrio of East Los Angeles. Finding our way backstage, we interviewed a Broadway chorus dancer after her performance in a hit musical. Getting to know these people, recording their stories and benefiting from their wisdom and hospitality has enriched our own lives beyond measure. Now, so many years later, we see these experiences as high points in our lives.

What we uncovered was astounding. Rich or poor, black or white, married or single, old or young, happy people all had something in common: *every one of them created happiness by making the same nine choices!*

The gift they gave us changed us in ways we could not have imagined, opening up a whole new world, a whole new way to be, to think, to live. It revolutionized the way we related to each other, the way we parented, our notions about friendships, our approaches to consulting, and our feelings about the value and richness in ordinary lives well lived.

To this day we remain students, not gurus, of happiness. But early in the process we knew we had to pass along the intelligence of this model. By 1996 we had already created and were conducting happiness workshops.

Since then, through training programs in corporations, hospitals and universities, in public workshops and keynote speeches, we have taught people from all walks of life—chiropractors, teachers, homemakers, psychotherapists, film makers, doctors, nurses, and even a state coroner—anyone interested in becoming happier. And, we've been guests on radio talk shows and television programs, and featured in articles in magazines and newspapers in a host of international publications.

The results have been remarkable. Even beyond the people with whom we've had "hands-on" contact, we have heard from readers and listeners all over the world who have changed profoundly as they integrate the nine choices. They have taught themselves how to build greater happiness into their lives.

Is happiness within your grasp? Yes. Have we created a tangible, clear guide to happiness? Yes. Can we make you happy? No. You have to make yourself happy. What we can give you is a portrait showing you how to grow, learn and change.

Who are the Happy People?

In our travels we've learned that our culture has a bounty of negative stereotypes about happy people. Perhaps you're skeptical too? For example, you might be thinking, "Are happy people so stupid that they don't realize how unhappy they should be? Don't these folks know that the world is not a happy place? Do they just hop out of bed feeling cheery every morning? Aren't they really 'Pollyannas'—in denial about sadness and pain?"

Truly happy people are certainly not in denial. In fact, they allow themselves to feel life's range of emotions deeply. They are not buoyant every minute of the day. In fact, one of the paradoxes of happiness is that, in order to experience life's greatest joys, we must sometimes experience its deepest sorrows. Happiness is a long-term emotional state that carries us through all our life experiences.

But aren't people happy as a result of personal circumstance? Doesn't it depend on money, security, relationships, where you live?

Actually, happiness doesn't come from any specific circumstance. The group whose stories appear in this book, and the many we've talked to thereafter, are extremely diverse. We found them in every socioeconomic level and every country we visited. They ranged in age from 16 to 101, and represented all races. They embodied a wide variety of belief systems, religions, and family backgrounds. Some were involved in long term relationships; others were single. Some were straight; some gay. Many had children; some did not. These are people you know.

The Proverbial Glass: Half Full or Half Empty?

One of the things that make these people special is their unique answer to the classic question: Is the glass half full or half empty? Their responses are what set them apart from the rest of us. Happy people will say the glass is both half full *and* half empty. Life is about coming to terms with both perceptions of the glass. Happiness is the result of our conscious responses to both the wonderful and the tragic components of life. They would tell you what creates a happy life cannot be reduced to a single cause—happiness is multi-faceted.

The nine choices of happy people are internal choices—unique tools they use consciously to enjoy life to the fullest and to move efficiently through difficulties and trauma. By following their hearts and minds, rather than allowing society to dictate how they should behave, they become special, charismatic people—the kind we want to know, the kind of people we want to be.

The Nine Choices

1. *Intention*— the active desire and commitment to be happy, and the decision to consciously choose attitudes and behaviors that lead to happiness over unhappiness.

2. *Accountability*— the choice to create the life you want to live, to assume personal responsibility for your actions, thoughts and feelings, and the emphatic refusal to blame others or view yourself as a victim.

3. *Identification*— the ongoing process of looking deeply within yourself to assess what makes you uniquely happy, apart from what you're told by others *should* make you happy.

4. *Centrality*— the non-negotiable insistence on making central to your life that which brings you happiness.

5. *Recasting*— the two-step process that transforms stressful problems and trauma into something meaningful, important and a source of emotional energy.

6. *Options*— the decision to approach life by creating multiple scenarios, to be open to new possibilities and to adopt a flexible approach to life's journey.

7. *Appreciation*— the choice to appreciate deeply your life and the people in it, and to "stay in the present" by turning each experience into something precious.

8. *Giving*— the choice to share yourself with friends and community, and to give to the world at large without the expectation of a "return."

9. *Truthfulness*— the choice to be honest with yourself and others, and not allow societal, workplace, or family demands to violate your internal contract.

Each of the nine choices made by happy people stands alone as an important and valuable life choice. But when they come together, they create a synergistic system. In other words, when they work as a whole their total result is far greater than the sum of their parts. And that synergy is what creates deep, long term happiness.

If you envision happiness as a wheel, the whole system becomes clear. In each of the subsequent chapters you will see how the choices flow logically, one to the next, from Intention to Truthfulness.

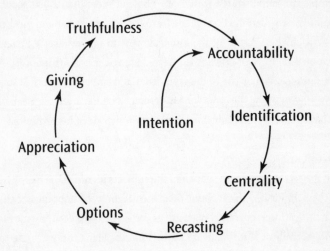

Our Methodology:
Finding and Studying Happy People

Most quantitative macro-studies on happiness find subjects based solely on a self-selection process. Whoever reports being happy is deemed an acceptable participant.

Our research methodology went a great deal further. We wanted to be sure we were talking with people who are exceptionally happy *over time*. We designed a comprehensive three-step process that first identified the interviewees and then qualified them.

STEP ONE:

We found a diverse group of happy people around the country by networking through our personal and professional contacts, and by asking complete strangers we met in our travels to identify the "happiest person you know." It seems that almost everyone knows at least one person who is extremely happy. And, in this referral step, we first affirmed that our interviewee might, indeed, be a happy person.

This initial inquiry brought us a remarkably diverse list. As an example, an acupuncturist with a client base of more than 1,000 people immediately identified one client, Caroline, a homemaker and mother of two children. A spur-of-the-moment query to a ticket-taker at Preservation Hall in New Orleans led us to Maurice, a jazz saxophonist. A business contact in The Netherlands led us to Hannah, a holocaust survivor living along the canals of Amsterdam. And the academic dean of a large university in California pointed to Tony, one of his professors.

STEP TWO:

In the second phase we contacted the subjects identified as happy by others and asked them about their own feelings of happiness. Self-identification is currently regarded as the single most accurate means of determining if someone is happy. Added to Step One, we began to feel sure of the validity of our test subjects.

Once our interviewees told us they were happy, we used in-depth, narrative interviews, known in the social sciences for their accuracy and depth. The actual interviews were candid discussions, without set questions, that lasted anywhere from an hour to half a day. Though the individual stories varied tremendously, happy people were quite articulate about their adamant choice to be happy and the behaviors necessary to live this happiness.

STEP THREE:

To qualify them further, we asked the subjects if we could talk to others in their social worlds in order to validate their self-perception of happiness. Whenever possible, friends, family, and colleagues verified the happiness of the interviewee by sharing observations and stories.

Numerous researchers have told us that our three-step approach far exceeds the selection and qualification process used in other studies of happiness.

The Control Group

Did we only talk to happy people? No. It was extremely important to be sure that happy and unhappy people are different, and to understand the differences in their responses during interviews. So, we set out to enrich our research with comparative references. We conducted a number of control interviews with people who consider themselves to be only somewhat happy or not happy at all. As you will see in upcoming chapters, the concerns, choices and behaviors of these two groups are dramatically dissimilar.

Happiness, History and Choice

Two critically important themes emerged repeatedly in our discussions with extremely happy people. First, you truly *can* choose happiness—it is not a matter of luck or happenstance. Second, happiness comes from within—you can't find it outside yourself. We believe, as do all of the people we've researched, that you have the power to create your own happiness. These themes will emerge constantly throughout this book.

The two ideas are not a result of New Age chic. The idea that our deepest happiness comes from within us has echoed for centuries throughout world literature and religion. No less a philosopher than Aristotle said: "Happiness depends upon ourselves." Marcus Aurelius wrote in Rome: "To live happily is an inward power of the soul." The religious texts concur. In the Bible, Jesus proclaimed, "The Kingdom of Heaven is within you . . . Seek ye first the Kingdom of Heaven and all things will be added unto you." This philosophy is also reflected in the two-thousand-year-old collection of Buddha's words, The Dhammapada: "The way is not in the sky. The way is in the heart."

That we can actually choose happiness is also abundantly discussed in the great texts. From Tibetan Buddhism we learn: "The student . . . can strive to furnish this relative world, his own creation, with things likely to lead to his own well-being, his happiness." The American forefathers had similar things to say about individuals being the source of their own happiness. Abraham Lincoln knew that happiness is independent of circumstance. He said, "Most folks are about as happy as they make up their minds to be." The nineteenth century philosopher Arthur Schopenhauer summed up the thousand-year-old discussion with a warning about relying on things outside ourselves to generate happiness: "Happiness belongs to those who are sufficient unto themselves. For all external sources of happiness and pleasure are, by their very nature, highly uncertain, precarious, ephemeral and subject to chance."

It is unlikely that the people we interviewed have read extensively on the subject of happiness. Choosing happiness is simply the way they live. But what we heard from them coincides with the thinking of some of the world's greatest philosophers and writers.

What You Can Expect?

This book is about choice in its most fundamental and creative form. Be prepared to be honest with yourself as you answer some key questions.

- What are the choices available to me?
- What will I get from each choice?
- Which choices reflect the person I want to be?

Expect to take a voyage of personal discovery in order to increase your awareness of the choices you make. Along the way you'll be able to look deeply into your heart and soul to discover how to create happiness. You'll be able to evaluate how you live, and to examine closely the kinds of choices you might make to become happier.

Don't expect profound change to happen overnight—it requires practice, study, a lot of self-evaluation and sheer honestly. Happiness has to do with the kind of personal authenticity that grows over time. As you read you'll be able to evaluate your inner self—your true desires, wishes and expectations—and to find ways to bring this to bear on your daily life.

How Happy Are You? Rate Yourself

Are you curious about yourself? How happy are you? Here's an opportunity to rate yourself. You can use the following "Happiness Inventory" to create your own picture of happiness. It is both descriptive and prescriptive, providing you with a view of where you are now, and giving you a sense of what you can do specifically to become happier. This scale is not designed to be an absolute instrument. Your score is unrelated to other peoples'. It is simply meant to be your personal point of reference as you read.

Happiness Inventory

Try to identify the way you feel physically and mentally at this moment. Do you feel content, centered, capable? Are you calm, oriented and rested? How deeply happy are you? Rate yourself:

1	2	3	4	5	6	7	8	9	10
Not at all happy									Extremely happy

1. Intention (Chapter 1) requires both the strong desire to be happy and the commitment. It is the fully conscious decision to choose happiness over unhappiness. As you go through your day, to what extent do you actively intend to be happy?

1	2	3	4	5	6	7	8	9	10
Never									Always

2. Accountability (Chapter 2) is the choice to assume full personal responsibility for our actions, thoughts and feelings, and the emphatic refusal to blame others for our own unhappiness. It is the insistence on seeing ourselves as having control over our own lives, rather than being at the receiving end of circumstance. To what extent do you assume personal responsibility for your life and take a proactive stance in the face of circumstance?

1	2	3	4	5	6	7	8	9	10
Never									Always

3. Identification (Chapter 3) is the ongoing process of looking within ourselves to identify what makes us happy. As you go through your day, to what extent do you ask yourself "Which choice or direction will truly make me happiest?"

1	2	3	4	5	6	7	8	9	10
Never									Always

4. Centrality (Chapter 4) is the happy person's non-negotiable insistence on making that which creates happiness a central activity in life. Happy people don't "wait to retire" or put off that which gives them greatest joy. To what extent do you centralize?

1	2	3	4	5	6	7	8	9	10
Never									Always

5. Recasting (Chapter 5) is the choice to turn problems into opportunities and challenges, and to recast extreme trauma into something meaningful, important and a source of life-giving energy. To what extent do you recast everyday problems by turning them into opportunity? Do you allow yourself to feel unhappy emotions deeply, and then move through sadness by converting trauma into opportunities and meaning?

1	2	3	4	5	6	7	8	9	10
Never									Always

6. *Options (Chapter 6)* is the decision to approach life by being open to any new possibilities, and of taking a flexible approach to life's journey. In your own life, are you aware of opportunities? Do you take risks? Are you flexible enough to jump into the unknown for the experience of trying something important or new?

1	2	3	4	5	6	7	8	9	10
Never									Always

7. *Appreciation (Chapter 7)* Happy people actively appreciate their lives and express gratitude and thanks to the people around them. They revel in each moment and transform that which is ordinary into something wonderful. To what extent are you aware of the moment and grateful to those around you for what they mean to your life?

1	2	3	4	5	6	7	8	9	10
Never									Always

8. *Giving (Chapter 8)* Sharing one's self with friends, community and the world at large without the expectation of a "return on investment" is a hallmark choice of happy people. Giving is a constant in life, and may manifest itself in one's profession, community work, or sharing through art. To what extent do you give richly of yourself to others?

1	2	3	4	5	6	7	8	9	10
Never									Always

9. *Truthfulness (Chapter 9)* Happy people "speak their truth" in an accountable manner, enforce personal boundaries, and will not con-

form to the demands of society, the corporation or the family whose demands violate their personal belief systems. Their truthfulness becomes a contract they have with themselves and, most important, it is a way to check their thoughts and actions against their own internal, personal code. How truthful are you with yourself?

1	2	3	4	5	6	7	8	9	10
Never									Always

What Do Your Scores Mean?

The inventory is meant to give you a personal reference point as you read, a portrait of the way you choose to be happy. Remember, statistically the scores are unrelated to those of other people. For example, your "6" reflects your view of yourself, and may mean something completely different relative to another person's "6".

The inventory becomes meaningful when you evaluate your own scores. Where did you score lowest? Highest? Were all your scores on the low side, or were most of them in the higher range, with just a few on the low side?

If you start by evaluating your lowest scores, you will pinpoint where you might start some personal work. These are likely the areas that will be most difficult for you to change.

The following chapters will explore in detail each of the nine choices of happy people. As you read you can expect to be moved by stores about people who have overcome extraordinary hardship. You'll also laugh at their mistakes and foibles along the way. Though the model you're about to discover is fundamentally about happiness, it's also about so much more: the quality of your relationships, success in your career, and your health.

Chapter 1

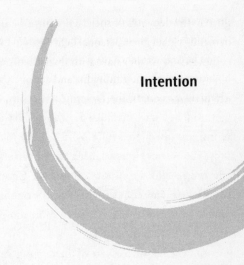

Intention

All of us who are happy have the intention of being happy. It seems to me that intention is the key.

Janet Jantzen, fund-raiser

Those who wish to sing always find a song.

Swedish proverb

The adventure of happiness begins with the intention to be happy, the most hidden, yet powerful choice we make. There's a reason that intention is at the center of the wheel of happiness. In our research and subsequent work with individuals and groups, intention is the force behind all happiness, the fundamental choice that drives the other eight. And here's why: Unlike most forces in life that are out of our control, our intention is fully in our control. In other words, we can't always choose our circumstances, but we can always choose our attitude and reactions to things around us. Unfortunately, in today's chaotic world, most of us fail to capitalize on that reality, and instead stumble from one activity to the next on autopilot—all because we are unaware of our intentions.

But whether we're aware of them or not, our intentions are driving the show. Minute by minute, they are the internal messages we give ourselves that dictate what we say, how we say it, and how we see things. This is why the happiest people in the world consciously set their intention before each event of the day. They understand that they have the power to choose a focus for each experience. And what they focus on is happiness.

The intention to be happy is a mindset that propels us toward living as happily as we can, predisposing us to make our days as joyful and significant as they can be. It's the point at which we stop responding unconsciously to the world around us and actively choose to be happy. We make a promise to ourselves, a commitment to happiness that becomes our compass, guiding the decisions we make and the actions we take.

If we don't truly intend to embrace happiness, we have unconsciously chosen something different. Without setting our intentions, even fleeting happiness is haphazard. But once we have intention firmly in place, happiness is no longer accidental, it is purposeful—something we are creating all day long.

The two of us have spent much of the last five years actively teaching people from all walks of life how to harness the power of their intentions to get the joy and invigoration they want, and to purposely craft their own experience of each event. If this seems unrealistic, let us show you how it works:

Setting Intentions All Day Long

You set your intention by seizing the fleeting window of opportunity that occurs between perceiving something and reacting to it. It is in these precious few seconds you actively choose your modus operandi—how you *plan* to be. Rather than responding reflexively, you choose your frame of mind in advance. You ask yourself the fundamental question: **What attitude will best enhance the quality of this experience right now?**

No matter what we're about to do, whether it's going to a baseball game, grocery shopping or even doing our income taxes, asking this question gives us the opportunity to shift from negative to positive feelings. Let's look at an example many of us have dealt with.

The Dinner Party

Suppose you are in the car on the way to a party at which you don't know a lot of people. For some of us this seems like walking into a social mine field fraught with booby traps and anxieties.

Our intention dictates the kind of evening we will have. We can clarify our intention by asking, "How do I want this evening to go? Is it my intention to worry about how I look, what I say, or what others are thinking about me? Do I want to spend my time being critical of others? Or, do I want to have the happiest time possible?"

To truly experience that happiness we need to let go of the mind-set that gets in the way. When we stop making negative judgments about ourselves and others, we can then focus our attention on fully engaging in the most enjoyable parts of the party. By repositioning our intentions toward the interesting social possibilities, developing new networks, sharing things about ourselves, learning something new, or making new friends, we are directing our feelings and actions towards a happy and satisfying experience.

Having helped people create happier lives for many years, we now clearly understand that the quality of our emotional experience is based almost entirely on the nature and strength of our intentions and very little on the actual things that happen in our lives. That's why happy people we found everywhere are purposefully finding opportunities to formulate specific intentions all day long. And, the more opportunities they find, the more they feel in command of their own destinies.

Let's turn to a situation that most of us would not be very happy about.

The Surgery

Richard, a tire salesman from Charleston, South Carolina, felt his normally sunny disposition plummet when he learned that he needed surgery to repair a double hernia. A week before the operation Richard's doctor told him that the day after the procedure Richard would probably ". . . hate his guts because the pain would be so intense."

> "My life is a series of deliberate mind-sets. Before I go into any discussion, or situation, I plant a seed in my brain. I take a moment to adjust my attitude, my tone of voice, body language, focus, and how I want to feel. But my first response to the idea of surgery was fear."

> "After a quick assessment, I decided that stress would only weaken my body. And fear had no positive outcome here at all. So I focused my attention on making my body as strong as possible and keeping my emotions positive."

The strength of Richard's intention drove all his subsequent behavior. Throughout the week Richard ate well, got plenty of sleep, and did deep breathing exercises. Just knowing that he was doing good things for himself brought joy and a sense of control.

Once Richard arrived at the hospital, he chose a specific set of intentions about the surgical procedure. He intended to find things to enjoy in the process, to approach the operation with humor, and most important, to be gracious and calm. Once again, his intention drove behavior. He joked with the nurses, watched with interest how the medical staff interacted with one another, and thought about how strong his body was. Given a choice, Richard elected to have a local-type anesthesia rather than a general, figuring he'd get to see what happened in the operating room. When Richard was wheeled into the O.R. the surgeon noted that he would be somewhat conscious so he got to choose the music they'd listen to during the surgery. He asked for something upbeat, so the doctor put on a salsa CD.

> *Some interesting things happened. First, I was supposed to be in the recovery room for two hours. Instead, all my vital signs came back so quickly I was discharged within forty-five minutes and got to go home. The doctor told my friend that I was the only patient he'd ever had who tapped his toes to the music during the operation.*
>
> *In keeping with my commitment to a positive experience, I had people come over the first night. I lay on the bed while we talked and played games. The pain was fairly intense but as long as I didn't laugh I was pretty much OK. Best of all, I didn't hate my surgeon.*

From the outset of our research, stories like Richard's brought together the compelling possibility that happiness and healthfulness are aligned. For this reason, applying the nine choices to health is the focus of all our long-term research. What we know for sure is that in the world of happiness, having strong intentions is the first step—the foundation of good things to come. How can we learn to be this intentional? Setting intentions throughout the day requires practice until it becomes almost as automatic as fastening your seat belt or brushing your teeth. Like so many other internal changes we decide to make, being aware and dedicated is the key to our success.

Happiness is an expression of the soul in considered actions.

Aristotle

Daily Intentions

Our world can seduce us into the negativity that's all around us—the constant demands we face, the troublesome people in our lives, the fragility of our uncertain world. For this reason, some of the happiest people start their day in a unique and affirming way. Rather than preparing the traditional "to-do" list of tasks, they put their energy into formulating an intention for the day.

Gloria's Story

During a consulting project at a large corporation, we were talking to the director of human resources about happiness in the workplace. When we asked him, "Who's the happiest employee here?" he instantly named Gloria. As we began to ask others the same question, her name surfaced time and again. On the day we finally met her, we knew why.

Gloria turns an interview over coffee into a memorable event. Her wry sense of humor and sparkle infuse every story she tells. How does she get through the aggravations we all deal with? Gloria makes intention a daily ritual.

*I love stories. Each morning, I tell myself a story about the kind
of day I intend to have. I actually promise myself a good day. The
story keeps me on track as my day unfolds. This is the single most
important investment of my time.*

Let's be realistic. No matter what our intentions, all of us occasionally have "one of those days" when it seems as if there's a con-
spiracy to make us *un*happy. In fact, Gloria's day had begun with a
medley of frustrating events. Her two teenage children took long
showers that not only emptied the hot water tank but threw them all
into morning overdrive. A jackknifed truck made the already heavy
commute traffic come to a virtual standstill. After she missed an 8
a.m. meeting, her boss let his displeasure be known to the entire staff.
And, midmorning, one of her biggest clients ran into a snag, which
required that she cancel plans for the rest of the day. Why, then, when
we caught up with her late in the afternoon was she in such high
spirits?

*My happiness depends on the story I tell myself. The facts are
the facts. What happened, happened. But I have a choice. I can
tell myself two kinds of stories about today.*

*The first is about how irresponsible the kids are, how horrible
the traffic is getting, that I've got a jerk for a boss, and there are
too many demands on me. But, in light of eternity, this isn't the
story I want to tell myself. This is the only day I've got. Why
would I want to have a bad one?*

*The story I tell myself comes directly from my strong
commitment to be happy. In this story the problems are still there
but I'm surrounding by people I love. I can cut the kids some
slack for being typical teenagers. I feel competent solving my
client's problems and appreciate the fact that I get to come in
contact with so many different kinds of people.*

When I tell myself the second story, I can stop, take a breath, and let all the negative stuff go. That's the great thing. Each day I have a new opportunity to be happy.

There is a notable difference between having the daily intention to be happy and just trying to get through the day. At first glance Gloria's story may seem like a normal reaction to a day's set of mundane events, but her process is far from typical. By adopting a story she wishes to tell herself, she is exercising our most fundamental choice—the right to respond to circumstances in the way we choose.

We have stories we tell ourselves about every part of our lives. Whether they're about the people we know, the problems we face or how we feel about ourselves, these stories are uniquely ours. And it is through them that we create our own realities. Sometimes, however, we are unaware that it is these stories, not actual events, that drive our feelings and actions. This is why it is so important that, like Gloria, we activate conscious intentions to monitor and modify these stories. This gets us what we want and allows us to be who we want to be.

Setting intentions is so powerful and dynamic because it can be used not only for simple issues like Gloria's, but for approaching the monumental, life-altering problems you'll also read about in this book. At the heart is the realization that even under dire circumstances, we always have choices.

We who lived in concentration camps can remember the men who walked through the huts comforting others giving away their last piece of bread. They may have been few in numbers but they offer sufficient proof that everything can be taken away from a man but one thing: the last of the human freedoms—to choose one's attitude in any given set of circumstances, to choose one's own way.

Victor Frankl, Man's Search for Meaning

The Lifelong Intention to Be Happy

We've seen that we can develop the intention to be happy for each situation, and also on a daily basis. But what about having intentions that are activated all the time? How do we create an ongoing intention to be happy? Where does a lifelong intention come from? Is it an inborn trait or something we can learn? As with all the nine choices of happy people, it is a learned behavior, and can be learned in many ways and at any time during our lives.

Though many people do not develop a solid intention to be happy until they are adults, for some people intention arises distinctly out of childhood experiences. For both Maddie and Max the intention came from a decision to choose happiness over unhappiness in the most difficult situations. Their stories are particularly compelling because they both experienced neglectful childhoods yet went on to become extremely successful and happy adults. The beauty of these two stories is that they provide us rare opportunities to see the moment when a lifelong commitment to happiness emerged.

Life in Hollywood

Maddie is a media personality in the Northeast who knows everybody in town—from the mayor to the captains of industry to the star players on the football team to her local mailman. When we asked her, "Who is the happiest person in this city?" she said, "Me!" Within a few minutes we were convinced. The same warmth that flows out over the airwaves is equally apparent the moment she walks into a room.

We immediately scheduled an interview for the next day. As she told us the story of her life, the contrast between the happy woman we saw before us and the unhappy childhood she described was remarkable.

Maddie's parents were part of the Hollywood elite of the early

1950s. She should have had an idyllic childhood, enjoying the opulent grounds of the mansion in which she was raised. But each new day in the lives of nine-year-old Maddie and her little brother, Carl, brought new uncertainties and fears. Their mother—alcoholic, drug-addicted and violent—periodically took an ax to the family Cadillac. As Maddie's mother's addictions took hold and her violent behavior increased, Maddie's father abandoned the family. Eventually, even the servants fled in the face of her unpredictable rages. Maddie and Carl were left alone with their disturbed mother who often didn't leave the house for days on end. Miles from the nearest market, they lived on peanut butter and tried to stay out of their mother's way.

> *My brother and I were usually by ourselves all day long. On school days, the bus dropped us off to a quiet and foreboding house. Some days we would hardly see our mother at all. We were so unhappy—almost numb.*
>
> *I knew the kids at school were different from us. I wanted to be like them. They were relaxed, they laughed and joked, and seemed to really enjoy their days. This was mysterious to me at the time. Then one day I said to myself, "I am going to be happy just like the other kids." I remember telling Carl I had it all figured out.*

Maddie could see that her mother was miserable compared to the other mothers she knew. She reasoned that the only way to be happy was to do exactly the opposite of what her mother did. She came up with an ingenious plan—to learn in reverse.

> *One day, sitting on the steps outside the vacant servants' quarters where we could hide out, Carl and I made a pact. We promised each other that we would find new ways to be happy every day. And each time we did—whether it was playing a new game, telling a new joke or having a good laugh—we would be different from her. This was a moment that will be etched in my*

memory forever. Carl and I still talk about it as the liberating
moment in our childhood.

Maddie and Carl challenged each other to look for every opportunity to create happiness for themselves. Their focus on seeking
happiness became an intrinsic part of their lives.

For most children, happiness is taken for granted. Because it is
an assumed component of family life, they don't actively spend time
imagining happiness or considering it or searching for it. But Maddie and Carl's vow to each other gave them a high degree of consciousness about happiness, and this awareness carried over into their
adult lives.

Creating happiness became part of our identity and set the
course for our futures. To this day, seeking every opportunity for
happiness remains a part of my daily life, and defines my
personality.

As difficult as their childhood circumstances were, Maddie and
Carl had each other. They drew the strength and courage to fight for
happiness from each other—and together they found it. But even
children who struggle alone through tragic childhoods can discover
the intention to be happy. Max was one such child.

My Kingdom of Happiness

As an infant, Max was consigned to the foster home system in rural
Minnesota at the close of World War II. His mother, an unwed
teenager from an impoverished family, hoped to take him back when
she finally married, so she refused to allow him to be adopted by a stable family.

Because he was not available for adoption, his only real value in
a foster home was as a child farm laborer. His biological mother
would appear periodically, promising him a "real" family, but her
promise was always broken.

Max's foster families were often violent, and he became the scapegoat for many of his foster siblings. His one joy was reading—something encouraged by a sympathetic second-grade teacher. Books offered an escape from the grim circumstances of life as he knew it and a glimpse of a better, happier world beyond the harsh landscape of rural Minnesota. At age eleven, Max had an epiphany:

> *Though it happened forty years ago, I remember the day as though it were yesterday. In school we were required to read* King Arthur and the Knights of the Round Table. *Arthur's kingdom was a wonderful world in which people intended to be honorable and trustworthy and good. In this kingdom people treated each other well and respected one another. Arthur had created such a happy place. I fell in love with his kingdom.*

King Arthur's world represented an alternate reality to Max. The eleven-year-old came face-to-face with intention:

> *I remember the moment when I thought to myself, "I can do this. I will lead my life as King Arthur led his." I had little in the way of value systems at that time and this seemed like such an ideal world.*

Max made a promise to himself never to stray from King Arthur's model. With no money to buy the book for himself, he stuffed it under his jacket and smuggled it out of the classroom. Keeping the book hidden in a secret drawer at home, he would reread it late at night, committing parts of it to memory. The book became his bible—a touchstone in his troubled life and his road map to a life beyond unhappiness.

> *Believe it or not, King Arthur has been my guiding light ever since. He was really a "people builder." I've brought as much of this into my relationships and my work as I can. I've chosen to live my life using what I learned from that book for over forty years and it still makes me happy.*

At fifty-two, Max continues to infuse the humanism of King Arthur's court into his professional life. Now a senior vice-president at a major corporation, he is known as a wise, generous employee-centered leader. (In Chapter 2 we will learn more about the impact of Max's childhood experience on his adult life.)

Like all happy people, Maddie and Max are highly conscious of their intentions to be happy. Whether we stumble on this consciousness in childhood or learn it systematically as adults, it is virtually required if we want to lead happy lives.

They seemed to come suddenly upon happiness as if they
had surprised a butterfly in the winter woods.

Edith Wharton

Trapped in an Unhappy World

There can be a reverse universe in the childhood world of happiness: a universe where unhappiness is rewarded. In such a world, aches and pains get top priority; laughing children are neglected in favor of children with problems. The idea that happiness might be a healthful and necessary part of family life has not been considered.

Like sixty-eight-year-old Dorothy, children who are raised in this kind of environment may never understand the intention to be happy. By the time Dorothy was born, her family had given up the possibility of crafting loving and warm relationships. Her parents inadvertently taught their five children that unhappiness would bring rewards. Throughout the many years we have known Dorothy, she has remained an unhappy person:

> *My parents were always overwhelmed with their own work and money problems. Unfortunately, the best way for any of us kids to get attention was to be sick or miserable or hurt. I think it was a trade-off: The more miserable I was, the more love I'd get. Even*

though my parents are long gone, the whole family still works
this way. I don't know how to change it.

Until Dorothy develops the intention to be happy, she will continue to attract people who support her unhappiness, as she supports
theirs. Indeed, her relationships are built on this shared unhappiness.

In her case, almost every discussion becomes a contest in negativity. Telephone calls and face-to-face interactions are based on com-
plaints. The unstated motive is to see who can "out-misery" whom.
If someone has a broken arm, another family member is sure to
match it and raise the ante with an impending operation. In this system, no one is outside the firing range of criticism about everything
from vacation decisions to choice of current spouse. Everybody's goal
is to cut down another person as a way to feel better about their own
unhappiness.

If she were to change, Dorothy fears that her entire support system of family and friends would pull away from her. It is actually the
fear of losing this familiar unhappiness that perpetuates her unhappy
life.

It's as though Dorothy has spent a lifetime creating her own
opera—and she is both impresario and diva. She's built the sets, written the libretto, composed the music and found the other actors. Unfortunately, the opera she has composed is a tragedy. And because she
runs the same production night after night, she sustains her own unhappiness. She feels stuck. Changing its entire theme would be a for-
midable task. She'd have to re-create everything from the ground up.

Dorothy's best choice would be to leave the theater and start
building another opera around a happier theme. But this option is so
overwhelming that, even with an adult's insight, Dorothy is convinced
that she has too much to lose. She has, in effect, given up the thought
of ever being happy.

But many people don't give up; they learn intention in their
thirties, forties, fifties and beyond.

Finally Finding Happiness

Adele, now fifty-three, remembers her strong desire for happiness as a child growing up in the Bronx. Once she hit her twenties she began following a traditional route—searching for the "things" she thought would make her happy.

> *I spent many years looking for what "it" was that would make me happy. I certainly tried many things. I've bought my share of clothes and household items I thought might make me happy. That's never done it. I've had successful businesses and I've had businesses that went bankrupt. That never did "it" for me. I tried relationships—for a long time I thought "it" was a relationship with a man. And I tried that over and over and that didn't work out.*
>
> *I did have fleeting moments of ecstasy. One of those moments occurred the night my restaurant opened. I remember looking around the room feeling the wonder of it—and how good it was that it had all come together. I had another one of those moments in my last marriage when I was lying in bed next to my husband after good sex and I thought, "This is the ultimate." And, of course, that wasn't lasting happiness. It was just a moment.*

Though she achieved a full measure of material stability, Adele's quest never resulted in the happiness she was seeking. With so many "things" and so little real happiness she was left totally unprepared for the traumatic loss of every one of those things.

As one of our first interviewees, Adele showed us early on that happy people don't necessarily live charmed lives. In 1991, she experienced an unusually tragic set of losses. Her life unraveled as the losses began to pile up.

> *In one horrible twenty-four-month period my life evaporated. I lost everything. My house burned down to the ground, leaving*

*me with nothing—no clothes, photos, furniture . . . no material
reminder of my previous life. During that time, both of my
parents died unexpectedly. My husband left me for a younger
woman at the same time that my restaurant went bankrupt. My
best friend moved to Seattle. Even the dog died.*

Every "thing" in Adele's life disappeared, and she had to make
decisions about how to go on. But without establishing some form of
intention, she would be immobilized. What were her intentions?

Having lost everything, Adele had many intentions to establish.
She explored the most fundamental of them—would she live or die?

*I had nothing. I was so filled with grief I thought maybe God
was somehow preparing me to die. Everything was gone, maybe
this was some monumental lesson in letting go, and that I should
let my life go, too. But as my initial shock began to clear, a feeling
that I wanted to live outweighed all of my thoughts about death.*

*I began to see there was hope among the ashes. There was one
big opportunity—I had a clean slate. As long as I had to start
over and create a whole new life, I was going to create a happy
one.*

*I wanted to feel whole. I was sure that I wanted to embrace
everything in life—the good and the bad. I wanted a feeling of
contentment, and to feel rested and gentle. I wanted to feel
unafraid—to feel I could handle anything that came my way.
And I wanted to feel this way for the rest of my life. In spite of my
grief, I could see that this all added up to happiness for a
lifetime.*

Adele intended to find a deep and enduring happiness. But, after
such incredible loss, how would Adele construct this new life? How
could she survive emotionally? She now had the intention to move
forward, but she was still overwhelmed by grief. (In Chapter 5, "Re-

casting," we will see how Adele successfully built a new emotional life and how she moved through the pain to emerge as one of our extraordinarily happy people.)

Early in Adele's recovery she had already learned something important: If we desire happiness, we can't rely on anything outside of ourselves to make us happy, whether it's a new car or a better love life. Even though our commercial world shouts at us that we can buy happiness, we know that it doesn't really work.

When we choose intention along with the other eight choices we can create happiness *from within*—true happiness that is lasting. The new car, latest promotion or community recognition may give us a momentary thrill, but the happiness that comes from within us is a profound sensation that endures. This is the kind of happiness we truly desire.

It is not easy to find happiness in ourselves,
and it is not possible to find it elsewhere.

Agnes Repplier

Creating Happy Kids

Having children can present the classic conflict between a personal intention to be happy and the intention to be a responsible and nurturing adult. Sometimes being happy as a parent seems to run contrary to the undisputed canon of good child-rearing: "The child comes first."

Almost all of us believe we can make our children happy—in fact, we assume it's our job. Our natural response is to give our kids what we think they need—to take them places, to expose them to culture, to fill their days with lessons and sports. We believe this will make them happy. But will it really?

Activities and toys bring our children enjoyment, which is wonderful. But enjoyment should not be confused with happiness. Just like their parents, the kids have to learn to create happiness from within. It's a process parents can teach their children.

As a single mother of three in the 1970s there was pressure on Betty to put aside her own happiness for the sake of the kids. But she didn't.

> *I had to support myself and the kids. I wanted to finish school so we could live better and, at the same time, be a responsible and loving mom. I knew I wouldn't make it if I neglected my own happiness. So happiness was my overriding focus.*
>
> *My personal goal was to live my greatest passions—motherhood, my own personal growth, friendships, being on a softball team and my love of animals. My goal regarding the children was to show them my love and acceptance. I was always empathetic, but never played the mother hen. My kids had to take care of one another when I was at school, they had chores to do, and they did without a lot of toys and designer clothes.*

This is intention. Even when things got tough Betty was determined to make a happy life for herself. Her intention flourished and her kids benefited from her example.

> *I don't believe parents can make their kids happy. The best thing we can do is model how they can make themselves happy. I've showed my kids, with my own life, that they have choices and can be responsible for making things happen for themselves.*
>
> *I never assumed that my children were there to make me happy. They knew I loved them for who they were, not who I expected them to be. I never blamed them for holding me back or slowing me down. I showed my kids I had control over my own happiness, and taught them that they deserve to be happy.*

What has become of Betty's children? Twenty-five years later all three live unusual, creative lives. One is a rancher, one a rodeo rider, and the third is a professional golfer. All are unconventional choices, but choices driven by the intention to be happy. Today, they are all parents.

I know I provided my kids with the skills they needed to be happy, but it still amazes me to see just how healthy and happy they are. And not only them, but my grandchildren as well.

Just as family traditions are passed down from generation to generation, so is happiness. Betty's grandchildren have inherited a legacy of happiness from her. Some people are not so lucky. Unfortunately, Victoria only inherited a large trust fund.

Why Aren't I Happy?

Victoria enjoys all the advantages of great wealth. Her opulent life allows her to travel extensively, shop where she wishes and enjoy the surroundings of her many homes. She has never suffered a moment's anxiety over financial insecurity. Victoria also has three healthy, intelligent children and a loving, concerned husband.

Anything but a snob, Victoria has spent a lifetime creating goodwill and helping others, using her money for socially responsible causes.

Most of us would love to have her life. But she is unhappy.

I'm actually angry at myself for being unhappy. I realize how fortunate I am, but I can't understand why I'm not content. I try to be a good person. I'm on five nonprofit boards. I just got a commendation from the city. I get loads of compliments and terrific strokes from my community work. I am living a wonderful life by everyone's standards. But I'm still miserable. Why isn't this working for me?

Victoria's primary intention is to please other people. This comes from a generations-old family pattern of social service and philanthropy. Her activities get her a lot of positive feedback, but it's external feedback.

Her reliance on others to make her happy won't work. No matter how many strokes she gets, it will never be enough. Regardless of her wealth, she doesn't give herself the gift of happiness. She depends on other people to give her that gift. When it doesn't come, she feels used and hostile. And even when she gets the approval she longs for, its effects are short-lived, and then she feels empty again. She has yet to learn that Victoria is the only person who can make Victoria happy.

Joy has nothing to do with material things, or with
a man's outward circumstance . . . A man living in the lap
of luxury can be wretched, and a man in the depths of
poverty can overflow with joy.

William Barclay

Janet and Arthur's Big Adventure

Janet and Arthur don't have a lot of money. What they have is an unusual relationship. Both of them are extremely happy people who found one another twenty-five years ago and have been married ever since. Their adventure put intention to the test.

Janet and Arthur both work at a private school. For three years they had been enthusiastically planning a trip to India. It was their dream vacation—six weeks during Christmas break in a fascinating and complex culture. The trip was a gift they were giving themselves after years of careful budgeting. They fully expected this adventure to transform their lives.

With passports in hand, they caught a Christmas Eve flight for New Delhi via Frankfurt. But someone had made a mistake. As they attempted to change planes in Frankfurt, they were shocked to hear that their visas were not in order.

After numerous calls to both the U.S. and Indian embassies, the couple was told that a trip to India would be impossible. They would have to spend Christmas night in Germany. That wasn't the only bad news—they were going to lose their substantial deposit on the New Delhi hotel.

Christmas Day found a tired and frustrated Janet and Arthur in a substandard Frankfurt hotel, standing in front of the window wearing their summer pajamas. Janet watched the snow fall on the cold and empty streets below.

The situation was tense—the kind of disaster that most of us have experienced in our relationships, usually with miserable outcomes.

> *I could tell that Arthur and I had the same thoughts. "Which one of us was responsible for checking the visas? Who confirmed the flights? This is so embarrassing—what will our friends think? Why is this happening to us?" I knew things were about to deteriorate rapidly. I had some quick choices to make.*

Under the same circumstances, most of us would make emergency decisions based on pragmatic considerations—the most sensible, efficient ways to solve the problem. But practical solutions sometimes overcome our intention to have the happiest experience possible. "Should we just give up and go home now—we've got six weeks and the house needs painting? Maybe we should stay for a week in Germany and then go home? Maybe we should cash in the India tickets and bank the money?"

What sets Janet and Arthur apart? Rather than pragmatics, they fell back on intention.

There's a word my mother used to use that has always stuck with me. The word is "mindful." I think the word says it all: full of mind. It's the way I want to be—full of intelligence and awareness. To me it means I'm not just reacting. I'm responding with forethought. And Germany was one of those situations where being mindful was an awful lot better than just blindly lashing out. . . .

So, I turned to Arthur and said, "We can either be angry and miserable or decide to take the high road and be happy. Let's make an agreement not to beat ourselves up. Let's not worry about the money. Let's not blame each other, the airline or the Indian government." I was still absolutely determined to have the trip of a lifetime—to learn about a whole new culture. Who said India was the only place we could do this?

With the intention to be happy driving their reactions, Janet and Arthur were able resolve the dilemma. Where else did Lufthansa fly that would fulfill their dreams? Where else could they immerse themselves in a new culture? Where else could they bask in the sun in their new summer clothes? Where else could they fly without a visa?

Where did they end up? Israel. The couple took off the next day for that ancient and exotic land, where they spent an unforgettable six weeks.

Janet and Arthur's friends still laugh about receiving postcards from Jerusalem that read:

Having a great time in "New Delhi." Wish you were here.

Shalom,
Janet and Arthur

Remember that happiness is a way of travel
—not a destination.

Roy M. Goodman

Getting Started

Choosing the intention to be happy is the beginning of our adventure. But intention is an attitude, not a behavior, making it sometimes difficult to master. Virginia, a university professor of English literature, attended one of our workshops for therapists and teachers. Several months later she provided us with a glimpse of her internal dialogue as she came to grips with her intention to be happy.

At the workshop she initially rated herself high on the intention scale. But as the day went on she realized that her intentions were not about *internal* happiness. These intentions were social conventions and expectations that had been ingrained in her as a child—impressing others, being a "good person," doing things the right way, being the perfect daughter.

> *I suddenly became aware that the intentions that had been driving me were not essentially important to me. After the workshop I made a decision to move toward happiness.*
>
> *For the next three weeks, my intention was to find out exactly what my intentions were! What decisions was I making throughout my day, and what was driving me to make them? Then I had to decide which of these intentions were important to me, not to other people. Once I knew for sure, I figured out a way to attach the intention to be happy to each of them.*

Let's refine Virginia's approach to explore our own intentions to be happy.

Learning Intention

1. Make a list of your most important intentions. Your list might include the following:

Long-term Intentions:

> I intend to be a supportive parent.

> I intend to spend a lot of time with my spouse.

> I intend to educate myself in a new area.

2. Evaluate your list. You might have four items, you might have twenty-four. Eliminate the items that are responses to other people's expectations or what you feel you "should" do. What you are left with are your most important intentions. These come from your heart.

3. After every item write the following phrase: ". . . and I intend to feel happy doing it." Your new sentence might read:

> "I intend to be a supportive parent . . . and I intend to feel happy doing it."

4. (This is the critical step!) Take a good look at the phrases you have written. Look deeply inside yourself and answer the following questions:

> How do I feel about these intentions? Do they feel real, authentic?

> Do these intentions match my previous approach to parenting, for example? Have I had the intention to be a happy parent all along?

If not, why haven't I had the intention to be happy? What have been the benefits of being unhappy? (Here are some clues: Have I built friendships around unhappiness? Have I been rewarded for unhappiness by my family? Have I understood how to make an everyday experience a happy experience? Or maybe I simply don't think about happiness when I make decisions.)

Without the intention to be happy, we can be seduced by the parade of unhappy events that life presents us. We're hurt by friends, stung by the loss of a lover, overcome by unhealthy habits or live at an inadequate economic level. But intention gives us the chance of stepping out of the parade. With that first critical statement, "I intend to be happy," we set ourselves on a course that will indelibly alter our lives.

Happiness is not a matter of events;
it depends upon the tides of the mind.

Alice Meynell

Chapter 2

Accountability

Intention

Here's my happiness philosophy in a nutshell:
I feel that I'm directly responsible for what
happens in my life.

   Mike Carr, electronics salesman

If you can bear a horribly mixed metaphor, I'd say
that I step up to the plate, rise above the fray and
bite the bullet, at which point I seek out a new
broom, and taking the bull by the horns, I then
play the cards I'm dealt—without crying over
spilt milk.

   Joan Hitlin, sculptor

Shallow men believe in luck, believe in
circumstance. Strong men believe in cause
and effect.

   Ralph Waldo Emerson

When we began our research we had some preconceived notions about what makes people happy. We fully expected happy people to tell us about loving relationships, having a good job and financial security. But something odd happened. We didn't hear anything about relationships, or careers, or money. Most people began the interview by talking about one central theme—their determination to take full control of their lives. This is what we call "accountability."

Accountability is how intention comes to life. If intention (Chapter 1) is an inner-driven desire to play in the ball game of happiness, accountability is its natural outcome—the urge to step up to the plate and hit the ball.

The word *accountability* can be misleading. Many of us associate it with being "called to account." This is a harsh cultural concept that says we must be responsible to an external authority. This interpretation is full of "shoulds"—mandates delivered from on high. Metaphorically, it's the tone of our mother's voice saying, "Why didn't you clean up your room like I asked?"

The brand of accountability that happy people talk about is quite different. It's a feeling that we are in charge of our own lives and that no one else has power over us. It's honoring our right to craft a life for ourselves that is rewarding, rich and exuberant. It's the assumption that no matter what life presents we have the ability to move ahead—to do something good for ourselves, to make a difference, to have an effect.

And why does this make us happy? Twenty-seven-year-old Mike gave us this great snapshot description:

> There's so much more joy in taking personal responsibility than in being a victim. I actively participate in my life. The buck stops with me! I trust I'm capable enough to handle anything that comes my way.

Happy people don't see themselves as victims, even under the most difficult circumstances. Their focus is on finding solutions to their problem and looking for what they can do to make their lives better.

There is a difference between accountability and responsibility. Although accountable people are responsible, responsible people are not necessarily accountable. Responsible people do all that is required of them—they pay the bills, take out the garbage, raise the kids, go to work, and follow the rules. In short, they are good citizens, and we admire them.

But that doesn't mean they're happy. Especially if, along the way, they're blaming the boss, complaining about the kids, and allowing external events to control the direction of their lives. Being responsible is important, but when we're accountable, we forge ahead, improving the quality of our lives by becoming proactive rather than reactive. We create our own circumstances, rather than allowing circumstances to dictate to us. As creators of our own lives, we are filled up. We feel content, capable and in control. The myriad of ways that happy people create their own lives is the theme of the rest of this chapter.

Happiness depends on ourselves.

Aristotle

Kathryn's Story—Part Two

(continued from the Prologue)

Being paid for sex with a stranger may have been my worst moment, but, as I look back on it, any of my problems could have become life-threatening. The bulimia, the promiscuous sex, my lifestyle in general. I was a crisis waiting to happen.

The thought that I was responsible for making myself miserable was slow in coming. But I finally got it. It came from a

*friend who painted this ugly picture of me—a poor sad victim
who was my own worst enemy.*

*The truth was, I had been using blame as an emotional
crutch—blaming my boyfriends for treating me badly, society for
my poor self-image, my parents for giving me false expectations.
But mainly I blamed Grandma K for ruining my life.*

*I'd been making the same bad decisions over and over, and
they kept getting me in trouble. I didn't want to do this anymore.
So I made the most positive step I'd taken in years. I joined a
support group for women.*

*That's when I first learned the idea of choice. The group
forced me to take on an entirely new perspective. I forced myself
to work under the assumption that I was actually choosing
everything in my life rather than having no choice at all. I saw
each event as something I had some control over. I looked at my
every move under a microscope. "How did I choose this? What
did I get by making that choice?" Most important, "What choice
is going to get me what I really want?"*

*Things were beginning to improve for me. My life wasn't as
stressed, but I still felt lost. I knew there must be something
better. What it was I didn't know.*

*Sometimes things happen that are "meant to be." I think it's
life offering you a chance to change. Or maybe in that moment
you're so ready to change that you're receptive. Anyway, one of
those moments happened to me.*

*Just at the point at which I was making better decisions, I
walked into a dance club for the first time. Fireworks went off
in my head. It was an unforgettable moment of clarity. The
glitter and lights and music. The spectacle of it. I longed to be
one of the instructors teaching the dance steps. I loved the whole
atmosphere.*

Everything changed for me that night. I felt my happiest

memories coming alive. For an instant I was that eight-year-old ballerina flying through the air. And as I twirled around the dance floor, I shook my parents and Grandma K's ghost right off my shoulders. I wanted to have that feeling of lightness forever. I made a vow to myself. Somehow, some way, dance would be part of my life.

This was the first time in a long time I really committed to something and stuck to it. I poured every dime I had into dance lessons. Each night I'd practice in my living room for hours on end. I was a natural. In six months I quit my job and became a full-fledged dance instructor. Within a year, I decided to go out on my own.

I printed up a few thousand flyers and handed them out downtown during lunchtime. Promoting myself was hard work, and the response was minimal. I could hear that little voice inside me saying, "Forget it, this is never going to work." But for the first time in years, I refused to blame the world. I just kept going.

After several weeks, I had signed up my first sixteen students and rented a dance space by the hour. When I wasn't teaching I kept looking for more students. It was the idea that I was "choosing" that kept me motivated. Even though I knew that many events were completely outside my control, just having the perspective that I had some areas of choice made all the difference.

I was on a roll. Word of mouth was bringing in more students. I even hired another dance teacher to work with me. But I was still bulimic, and I knew that if I was to be really happy, I needed to deal with everything getting in my way. This was something I couldn't do on my own, but with a lot of professional help and hard work, I eventually beat it.

I was beginning to feel optimistic. I had started a business. I

*was regaining my health, treating myself better. I had stopped
blaming my family for my problems. Things were looking good.
But, believe me, there were still lots of bumps in the road ahead.*

(To be continued in Chapter 8)

The Blame Game

Of the many behaviors that characterize happy people, one stands out
resoundingly. Happy people avoid blaming in all its incarnations.
They don't blame other people, they don't blame circumstances, and
they don't blame themselves. To happy people, blame serves no purpose. It doesn't ever get us what we truly desire.

In fact, our research clearly shows that blame, along with its
family members—greed, envy and jealousy—are among the most
dramatic indicators of unhappiness. These reactions lead nowhere.
They are only ways to dodge responsibility. Except for the brief sense
of satisfaction that comes from pointing a finger at someone else,
blaming ultimately leaves us stuck with feelings of resentment.

The choice to be accountable is the choice to be masters of our
own fates. As such, we choose to respond to our real emotions—love,
anger, sadness, joy. How do we find these authentic feelings? By looking at "my part."

My Part

Picture this setting: two friends sitting in an outdoor café, sharing
their problems. One is not happy. In fact, she's just had a falling-out
with a colleague. She believes she's been mistreated, and she feels betrayed, angry and even a little self-righteous. As she explains the situation to her friend, she catalogues the ways her colleague offended
her. "You won't believe what she said to me. Wait 'til you hear what
she did."

In an effort to feel better about herself, our unhappy person is focusing all her energies on her treatment by the other person. But she hasn't gained any new insight into herself.

Now imagine the same setting: two close friends talking over a cup of coffee. This time, the friend with the problem is a happy person. If you could listen in, you'd hear a very different conversation. Our accountable friend would be just as angry or upset, but she'd approach the situation differently. "What was my part in this situation?" she'd ask. "What did I do? How can I change things? What can I learn from this experience?"

This dialogue is not self-blame. Rather, it's a mature look at what we can realistically change in our lives. It's a way for happy people to control their own destiny. And it's a way to gain deeper understandings of our feelings and motivations.

When we answer the question "What's my part?" we feel better, happier. Why? Because we are addressing the only thing we can affect—ourselves. We give ourselves the power to move through the situation, rather than being bogged down by trying to get the other party to change.

Focusing on "my part" after we've been attacked may seem counterintuitive. But this is what happy people do.

Let me listen to me and not to them.

Gertrude Stein

Valerie and the Unaccountable Accountant

Valerie, the humorous, successful owner of a catering company, was referred to us by a food critic we know who labeled her the happiest person he'd ever met in all his travels. With a recommendation this glowing, we knew she was someone we had to meet. After tracking her down in the Knightsbridge section of London, we talked with her for hours over tea, toast and tiramisu in a neighborhood bakery. The subject was accountability.

Six months previously, Valerie had dealt with a major challenge when she fired Jackie, her once trusted in-house accountant, for embezzlement. After a long investigation, it became impossible to deny that Jackie had forged checks, stolen from petty cash and ultimately caused a $30,000 shortfall in company profits.

Most of us would see Valerie as a noncontributing victim of Jackie's crime. But was she?

I had a couple of choices here. I could concentrate on Jackie's behavior or look at my own. The money was gone, and so was Jackie. Railing at her any further would have been a waste of time.

I knew that as Jackie's employer, I must have played a major role in this episode. Even though it was an unintentional role, I had to figure out how I could stop something like this from happening again.

After a lot of soul searching, I came to some hard realizations. I hadn't set appropriate limits for my employees or given them a code of professional expectations.

In being unaccountable to herself, Valerie had ultimately been unaccountable to her employees and the business. She'd designed ineffective business systems, notably inadequate bookkeeping practices without built-in checks and balances.

As a result of her self-evaluation, Valerie changed her business systems. Even more important, after finding out *what* had happened, she tried to figure out *why* it happened:

I had desperately wanted to create a cozy family atmosphere at work. I think I actually cared more about being loved than about myself and the business. This was a pattern I had learned from my mother. I never had clear limits as a child, and so I failed to set them for my workers. Deep down I knew something wasn't right, but I closed my eyes to the things going on around me. I was trying to be everyone's mother.

When we're truly accountable to ourselves, and go beyond *what* happened to discover *why* it happened, we begin to uncover underlying emotional and behavioral patterns that don't serve us well. Finding these underlying causes led Valerie to a much more comprehensive set of solutions. She not only designed new business systems and personnel policies, she took the opportunity to become aware of, and then change, an old family pattern. This is where the real benefit came. Without this kind of fundamental change, Valerie would be continually vulnerable to this type of problem.

It is a painful thing
To look at your own trouble and know
That you yourself and no one else has made it.

Sophocles, Ajax, *c. 450 B.C.*

The Affair Was All Her Fault

James graciously agreed to an interview after becoming fascinated with our research. Although he'd like to be happier, at sixty-eight, James is a bitter man who feels manipulated by his wife. After twenty secretive years, he persists in justifying the affair he's still hiding from his wife, Dena.

> *This affair would never have happened if Dena had been more interested in sex. She's cold and competitive, a put-down artist with an acid tongue. She's been yelling at me for thirty-five years. Believe me, I've done the best I could—I never yelled back. The only way I could survive was to tune her out.*

James sees himself as the damaged party, not Dena. He feels she has mistreated him, and blames her for pushing him into the arms of another woman. Ask James if he might, in fact, have played some role in the situation, and he can't see it:

> *Dena's so difficult we could never discuss any of this. Any time I*
> *tried to talk to her about changes in the relationship, she made it*
> *impossible. What was I supposed to do?*

Rather than taking any proactive steps toward making things better, James *colludes* with Dena in perpetuating an unhappy life for both of them.

How is he colluding? He claims to be a passive recipient of Dena's behavior, but, in reality, he's actively involved. James's passivity is a camouflage for unaccountability. He is passively allowing a bad situation to continue without intervening. He is withdrawing from dialogue that might make things better. But most of all, he's dishonest, purposefully withholding information that would allow Dena to make fully informed decisions about her own life.

> *I don't think Dena would want a relationship with another*
> *man anyway. This is how she wants to live. Anyway, she's*
> *proved my point. . . . Every year she becomes more and more*
> *distant.*

It's as if James is playing a game of poker with four aces up his sleeve. His secret information controls the entire course of the game and the fate of all the players: Dena, James and his lover. In spite of his enormous influence over the situation, James still believes that it is Dena who has dealt him a bad hand.

These are three people caught in a tragic web of blaming, misconceptions and false expectations. Even though James sees himself as powerless, he's the one who has held the power for years. If he had been accountable and told the truth, he would have allowed all three of them the possibility of creating a happier life. Certainly, his own life would have been happier.

Take your life in your own hands and what happens?
A terrible thing: no one to blame.

Erica Jong

Defending Yourself

James blames his problems on his wife so that he won't have to accept responsibility for his own unhappiness. His defensiveness blinds him to the truth of his life.

We all have defense systems—protective strategies that we adopted as children. These defenses are emotional walls we built once upon a time in an attempt to protect ourselves against assault from people older, bigger and more powerful than we were. The higher the walls, the less vulnerable we felt.

As adults we still have some of those same tender spots. And we've added some new ones along the way. There are many times we still feel vulnerable and respond by invoking our defenses.

Do these old strategies really protect us? Do they keep us safe? Very often they just get in our way. Now the walls tend to imprison us. Habitual holdovers from the past, defenses limit our choices, impede our responses and often make it impossible to hear, let alone utilize, valuable feedback. They are keeping us away from relationships, ideas and possibilities which are components of a happier life.

There are all kinds of protective strategies that people adopt and unconsciously hold on to. Most of us find it easy enough to recognize them in someone else's nonaccountable behavior. Some examples:

• A coworker who lashes out in anger to camouflage mistakes.

• Your spouse who retreats into deadly silence when confronted with an uncomfortable topic.

• The teenager who pretends not to understand as a way to skirt the issue.

• Your boss who always has to be right rather than admit you might have a better way.

Most of us spend a lifetime perfecting our defenses. When we feel threatened, angry or vulnerable, we break into them easily, using them when other choices would be more accountable. Why? They are so ingrained in us that they become automatic reactions. Until we develop awareness, we haven't given ourselves a choice.

In times of duress, happy people gravitate toward openness rather than defensiveness. This takes the form of honesty, intimacy and a willingness to be vulnerable. They move away from negative judgments of people and focus on being receptive and compassionate to others. Our own experience in meeting these people illustrates this point. When we called them, they frequently had no idea who we were, yet, rather than meeting us with suspicions, they welcomed us with warmth and a spirit of generosity.

Still, none of us are completely defense-free. However, if our drive is to be happy we need to reduce our defensiveness. The extent we do so is the degree to which we are finally free to fully experience the richness and texture of our life and the people in it.

The next exercise will give you an opportunity to become more conscious of the defenses you may have perfected through the years.

The Defenses

The following list is a collection of some of the most commonly used defense strategies. We've used it over the years while teaching teams to address breakdowns in communication. Among the most fascinating groups are well-defended senior corporate executives. What starts as a quiet conversation about behavior at work typically develops into a lively analysis of personal lives and the role of defenses in marriages, friendships and relationships with children.

Sometimes just talking about defenses can make us more open and less defensive. Take a look at the list and try to identify the defenses you use most often.

1. Loss of humor
2. Taking offense
3. High charge or energy in the body
4. Playing dumb
5. Needing to be right
6. Wanting the last word
7. Flooding with information to prove a point
8. Endless explaining and rationalizing
9. "I'm a victim—poor me!"
10. Teaching or preaching
11. Rigidity—"I'm not willing to change"
12. Denial—"There's no problem"
13. Withdrawal into deadly silence
14. Cynicism
15. Sarcasm
16. Making fun of others
17. "It's just the way I am!"
18. Being highly critical
19. Withdrawal from negotiation
20. Blaming others
21. Sudden onset of illness
22. Confusion
23. Sudden fatigue
24. Acting crazy—the temporary insanity defense
25. Intellectualizing
26. Eccentricity
27. Being too nice
28. Hearing only what I want to hear
29. Counterattack
30. Holding a grudge
31. Trivializing with humor
32. Inappropriate laughter
33. Sour grapes—"I didn't want it in the first place"
34. "I'm already aware of that"
35. Self-deprecation

Once you've read through the list, answer the following questions:

Is there a payoff in using your defensive strategies?

> When do you use them most frequently?
>
> What behaviors in others seems to trigger these responses?
>
> Think of a situation where you responded defensively:
>
> How could you have substituted accountable responses for defensive reactions? Could you have been more open, listened more actively, disclosed more about yourself?

As we've said before, it's within our power to choose how we want to be. We can be rigid in our opinions and insist that we're right, or we can be open and search for the truth. We can choose to withdraw and keep people away, or we can be more vulnerable and let others know who we really are.

When happy people catch themselves becoming defensive, they ask themselves: Is this how I want to be? Is this really the response that's going to work the best?

Most of the time, the answer is no.

Liz Listens

At thirty-five, Liz is a married mother of two who still gears up mentally before any interactions with her parents and two older sisters. This family specializes in two conflicting defenses: shouting and not listening. Having honed their defense formula over many decades, they make every issue a contest of wills. Their tried and true technique is attack. They wear down their opponents by flooding them with information. The rationale is: If I'm the last one talking, I win.

But Liz has a secret weapon. "We can't figure it out," laments Liz's sister, Joan. "For some reason Liz is the only person in our family who gets along with everyone else."

What's Liz's secret? Long ago she gave up the need to be right and chose to remove herself as a contestant in the family competition.

I love my sisters dearly, but they are at their worst when we have to make decisions. Planning our parents' fiftieth wedding anniversary was no exception.

When we got together, each sister had her own opinion about what should be done, who should do what, who should be invited, et cetera. They immediately started cutting each other off and attacking each other's ideas. This is the point when I made the conscious decision not to join the attack.

I've learned to replace my urge to attack with a more compassionate approach. I really listen and try to understand what they want by temporarily putting aside my own judgments. They've got their ideas, I've got mine.

When my sisters finally stopped shouting, I did something that surprised them. I asked for even more information. It's hardest to ask for more when I feel defensive and vulnerable. But I know that's when I most need to ask.

How can asking for more in a hostile situation make Liz happier? It sounds like she's a glutton for punishment.

By listening openly, Liz reduces her sisters' need to attack. They feel heard, are willing to lower their guard, and Liz begins getting information that is honest and accurate. The tension level in the room drops. Quieter, more reasonable conversations take place. Most important, when the sisters finish they're open to hearing what Liz has to say.

I'm careful not to blame them or tell them they're wrong. I just talk about my own opinions, and why they're important to me.

This is the ultimate form of accountability. Liz takes responsibility for her own feelings about the situation and about herself. Notice that Liz, not her screaming sisters, empowers the situation.

Her sisters still haven't figured it out. All they know is that they love being with Liz. It's the only time they get anything accomplished.

Overcoming Omnipotent Responsibility

Liz nurtures a loving, warm family system by letting down her defenses, without feeling that she needs to assume responsibility for her sisters. She listens, makes agreements and sticks to them. Her communication is clear, open and honest. She doesn't assume that anyone can read her mind, and at the same time she lets her sisters be who they are.

Accountability to others is *not* about codependence, playing God or taking on inappropriate responsibility for others. It's about insisting they be accountable for themselves. Assuming "omnipotent" responsibility for people who are capable of being responsible for themselves undermines the integrity of our most important relationships—at home and at work.

King Arthur at Work

In Chapter 1 you were introduced to Max, who learned "intention" as a little boy from the legend of King Arthur. Now as an adult, living in New England, he continues to use King Arthur as his guide, both personally and in business.

Max is considered the most successful manager in his nationally known company and is destined to become its next CEO. But he's an enigma. In spite of the fact that he's the most demanding division head in the company, his employees love him. Even though theirs is the most productive division, they have much more fun than any other unit. Month after month they exceed performance expectations. Max spends less time in the office than any other senior manager, but his group shows the highest profits.

What's the key to his success?

I've got different objectives for my team than any other manager. They're based on getting excellent results through personal responsibility. My cardinal rule: Nobody is allowed to blame anyone else. We've all agreed there's no gossip, back-stabbing, making excuses and complaining without looking for solutions. If you're blaming someone, you're looking backward. It is impossible to look backward and forward at the same time. My focus is on learning from the past to make the future better, not on punishing someone for what happened. It's a waste of time.

I've been to a million seminars on leadership training. I still think King Arthur had the best technique. His job was to create an environment that encouraged the growth of his knights.

My role on the team is to be clear, honest and straightforward. I make myself available to anyone who needs my help. But, if I do their jobs for them or "cover" for them when they make mistakes, I'm taking responsibility for them. This cripples them.

The result: We trust each other. It's the mortar that binds the team.

The key to Max's productivity is his accountability to himself and the expectation that his employees will also be accountable for themselves. They all reap the benefit of a trusting, frictionless team in which everyone feels supported and there is no time wasted on fear—worrying about being scapegoated, not having enough information, being distracted by someone talking behind other people's backs. Max has a happy team because he's got an accountable team.

Happiness Is Hell for Victims

Happiness is not easy when life gets tough. Staying accountable can be difficult when we are on the receiving end of a frustrating or sad circumstance. It becomes even more difficult in the face of tragedy. Although it is likely we truly are victims under these circumstances, positioning ourselves as such seriously undermines our chance of regaining happiness.

We don't have to be victims. If we refuse to accept that role, even the most unfortunate among us have the potential of taking extraordinary steps on our own behalf. Happy people who have been hurt often courageously change the circumstances in which they find themselves. This is the case in the final three stories of this chapter.

Hannah and the Nazis

We interviewed Hannah in her three-hundred-year-old row house on the Princengracht, a gently curving canal in the heart of Amsterdam, The Netherlands. Every room is crowded with paintings, each with a special story of its own. An optimistic and gracious widow in her mid-seventies, Hannah is a retired physician as well as a proud mother and grandmother. Hannah's warm countenance belies her experiences as a Jewish teenager during World War II.

When the Nazis swept into Holland, Hannah, as the youngest child, was sent to live with family friends in Belgium. Within days her parents and brother were rounded up and transported to the concentration camps. Throughout the war Hannah risked her life in the Belgian underground, never knowing the fate of her parents or her dozens of aunts, uncles and cousins. When the horror was over, most of her extended family, including her father, who was deported to Auschwitz, never returned.

Would anyone argue that Hannah has been a victim of extraordinary cruelty? How does someone live happily after such a tragedy? What makes it possible for Hannah to play the piano she "inherited" from a cousin who never returned from the camps, without aching for revenge?

> *These events were so horrible, so traumatic that it took me a number of years to reconcile my feelings about them. But I never considered myself a victim of what happened during the war. Certainly, I have been terribly hurt. I felt extreme sadness, pain and loss. But carrying around a feeling of victimhood? No, that would do nothing more than keep such horrors alive.*
>
> *I will not allow myself to be enslaved by the past. From the start, my interest is in positive ways to ensure that this will not happen again. Being a victim, blaming the Nazis, is not one of them. . . .*

We might question Hannah's attitude, believing that expressing blame and resentment in this circumstance would be healthy, appropriate, even therapeutic. She has suffered. Hasn't she earned the right to feel victimized?

> *Listen. My family has lived peacefully in Amsterdam for more than four hundred years. Allowing five atrocious years to ruin my historical memory of the other 395 would be a personal tragedy. Feeling that I'm a victim of the Nazis gives them a perverse power over me. It would keep me in their hands and allow them to continue damaging me and my family fifty years later. Letting go leads to happiness.*

If Hannah's attitude toward the Nazis surprises you, consider this: What damage might she have done to her family had she held on to a feeling of victimization? Would her attitude have affected the security and well-being of her children? Could she have built a loving, enjoyable married life? Could she have been both a victim and a successful physician? Living well and happily was the result of assuming power over her existence—taking back her life from her tormentors.

Accountable in Alabama

If Hannah's extraordinary life in exotic Amsterdam seems remote, consider Jerry's quiet small-town life in rural Alabama. On a car trip through the Deep South, we stopped for lunch and asked the locals who was the happiest person in town. Jerry was the unanimous choice. He also turned out to be a surprising choice, particularly after we heard his life story.

Like Hannah's, Jerry's home is a visual autobiography. The walls are filled with generations of family photos and mementos, from yellowed newspaper clippings of his parents' fiftieth wedding anniversary to pictures of his own exploits as the high-school quarterback during the early 1950s.

Both Jerry and his wife grew up in this town, as did their parents. Together they built a family business that supported them and their four children. Jerry is very proud of his life. He has made deliberate choices to ensure his happiness, doing the things he loves most with the people he loves most. An active member of a half-dozen community organizations, he counts his blessings on a regular basis.

In 1988, Jerry's picture-perfect life came apart. Steven, his youngest child, was killed on a country road by a drunk truck driver who swerved out of control.

The death of a child seems unimaginable to any of us. And in a quiet community, where this traffic fatality was the first on record, Steven's death was especially shocking. Still, Jerry chose not to blame:

> I could never have imagined the pain I feel. But blame, no! I've never been in the business of assigning blame. That's the job of insurance companies.
>
> I'm a father who lost a child. My job was to heal myself and

my family. I had to find some meaning in this tragedy and
to take measures so that this will never happen to anyone
else in town. I had a lot to do, just surviving this. Blaming
would have diverted my attention away from the real tasks at
hand.

The tasks at hand were to grieve and to heal, and Jerry slowly worked through his terrible sense of loss. Realizing the ephemeral and precious nature of life, Jerry and his wife eventually began to take better advantage of their time on earth. They would leave the business for several months each year, going off on exotic vacations all over the world. They now count among their friends people in Venezuela, Thailand and Morocco.

Jerry still grieves for his lost boy; he cried openly during our interview. But rather than shutting himself off from the world in a haze of bitterness, Jerry has been motivated by Steven's death to reach out. (Jerry's delicate process in moving through this tragedy will be discussed in Chapter 3.)

Blaming Your Body

There are few more devastating experiences than a life-threatening illness. This is when we feel most vulnerable. Betrayed by our own bodies, we often blame ourselves. But, by blaming ourselves, we become our own victims. What form does self-blame take?

- Maybe I "willed" myself the disease?

- Perhaps I wouldn't have cancer if I'd eaten more broccoli.

- If only I'd reduced my stress level this wouldn't have happened.

If it seems impossible to hold on to happiness in the face of a serious illness, blaming ourselves makes happiness even more elusive.

What we most need is a sense of capability and centeredness. A proactive attitude is vital for creating these feelings.

At the time of our interview, Patricia was recovering from a radical mastectomy, followed by chemotherapy and radiation treatments. From the onset of the disease, this beloved and much-respected mayor of a college town in the upper Midwest had been open with her constituents about her illness. Everyone was cheering her on.

Her initial prognosis had been frightening: a comparatively fast-growing cancer of the breast with possible metastasis. But now things were looking up, and the doctors were predicting a full recovery.

> For a fleeting moment, I flirted with the notion that I had somehow caused the cancer. But then other emotions surfaced: hope, curiosity, anger, energy.
>
> What I really wanted was to go through this with a feeling of optimism—the belief that my treatment would be successful regardless of my fears. This was how I could be responsible to myself.
>
> I handled breast cancer by saying: "My body belongs to me, not to the doctors." I insisted on participating in every discussion of my case and making the final decisions about my course of treatment.
>
> I did a lot of research and tried to learn as much about the problem as I could. I spent hours in the library and on the Internet. I searched out as many experts as I could find. I joined a support group for women with breast cancer. And I huddled with my husband for days on end, discussing possibilities and solutions. Finally, I spent time alone soul-searching.
>
> I didn't waste a day feeling sorry for myself. Difficult periods happen to everyone, and this has been difficult for me. I didn't expect it and I certainly didn't want it. But I have lived it fully. Not one part of my life has been lost—feelings, experiences, decisions, risks—it's all mine. I own it, I accept it, and I feel

fuller and healthier for having gone through this on my own terms.

When we assume complete control over a situation, we feel most competent. We have done the best we could possibly do for ourselves. We have left no stone unturned. And we have given ourselves the freedom to experience fully our fear, sadness and anger as well as our hope and joy.

There is ample medical research supporting the idea that patients who feel a degree of personal control over their illness reap certain benefits. They have greater success with medical treatment, they heal better, and they are happier. Clearly, personal accountability affects our physiologies. Behavior affects biochemistry.

Assuming we have the intention to be happy, and we want to be accountable to ourselves, how do we discover what will truly make us happy? As you will see in Chapter 3, you can use a deeply personal technique—identification—to find out.

Self-pity is our worst enemy and if we yield to it,
we can never do anything wise in this world.

Helen Keller

Accountability

Intention

Identification

Identification

How do I stay happy? I listen to my heart.

Paul Hardin, accountant

Ordinary riches can be stolen; real riches cannot.
In your soul are infinitely precious things that
cannot be taken from you.

Oscar Wilde,
The Soul of Man Under Socialism, 1891

Some people *tell* us how to be happy; others *sell* us how to be happy. But this is their notion of happiness, not ours. We're bombarded with these versions of happiness by our family and friends, our institutions and the media.

To make the next choice beyond accountability, we decide for ourselves what makes us happy. This requires an act of supreme kindness to ourselves. It's loving ourselves enough to reach down into our souls and identify our needs, aspirations, interests and passions. It's having enough self-esteem to say, "This is what I need," and giving ourselves priority over those who would ask us to conform to their idea of happiness.

This act of self-affirmation is the process of identification—the choice happy people make to figure out what makes them truly happy. They don't dance to the happiness messages others send them: buy this product, join this club, follow this ideology. Rather, they look deeply within themselves to envision what will make them happiest in a given situation. They don't do it occasionally or only when something big happens. The happiest people—people like Peter—do it as a matter of course, every day of their lives.

If you do not ask yourself what it is you know, you
will go on listening to others and change will not come
because you will not hear your own truth.

Saint Bartholomew

Turning Life Around

Peter is energetic and enthusiastic. He wakes up each morning with great anticipation about his day. But it wasn't always this way. He remembers one spring morning not too many years ago, when he was walking with his father along the Delaware River confiding his feelings of discontent.

My life isn't working. I've got to change something but I don't know what.

My father told me, "You've always wanted what you don't have. For you, Peter, the grass is always greener on the other side. Take a look at your life! You've got a high-paying job, a great wife, beautiful daughter, more toys than you can shake a stick at. You've got an ideal existence."

I couldn't argue with my father's opinion. I felt selfish. With so many things to make me happy, I felt I had no right to complain. But when my dissatisfaction didn't go away, I began to ask myself questions. At first, they were the typical ones: What do I need to be more successful? What new goals can I set for myself? What else can I buy that might make me happier?

I gave myself the usual answers—with the usual results. I became more successful at work, and rewarded myself with a new car. But the thrill was short-lived. There was something missing. So I kept asking questions.

One day I stumbled on a new, much more personal question: "What makes me really, authentically, honestly, deeply, personally happy?"

This new question prompted new answers—answers which had nothing to do with money, toys or what I thought of as success. They had to do with senses, experiences, aesthetics, emotions and activities which speak to who I am as a person.

Peter's answers included simple things like eating fresh apricots, watching the sunrise, swimming, listening to 1920s jazz. He discovered more intimate items as well: discussing historical novels with friends, cooking dinner with his wife, hiking with his brother. He also honed in on the parts of his law practice that he most enjoyed—the political advocacy, the environmental law cases he'd taken on, the times when he was able to provide emotional support for his clients.

*I could see and feel these things in my mind's eye. Some of
the things I came up with I hadn't thought about in years—
like fly fishing. Others, like cooking dinner with my wife, I
realized I hadn't done in months. Best of all, I was overwhelmed
by a sense of relief—I had found answers that meant something
to me.*

Peter discovered what all happy people know—that what makes
him happy is uniquely personal. No two answers to happiness are
alike because no two people are alike. The secret is to keep asking the
questions.

*Several times each day I ask myself, "What would make me
happy right now, right at this minute?" And every time I ask
myself the question I get happier. It's a way for me to be tuned
into myself without being critical of myself. This allows me to
accept myself just as I am.*

*Things, even people, can change, but my questioning allows
me to stay connected to myself, the real me. It's also allowed me
to let go of a lot of things that are not really important to me
anymore.*

Sometimes we're so busy responding to other people's formulas
for happiness that we haven't created a formula of our own. Like
Peter found, this can be the crucial difference between our long-term
feeling of happiness and a sense of frustration and emptiness.

Here's a way to give identification a try:

Creating Your Dream List

Working with identification during workshops and corporate
training sessions has provided astonishing insights. Simply ask-

ing the question "What really makes me happy?" has brought about profound change for many people.

For this exercise you will need: a comfortable and quiet place to write, writing implements and a timer.

1. Ask yourself: How do I feel physically right now? Do I feel elevated, depressed, anxious, happy? Make a note of your feelings.

2. Set the timer for four minutes.

3. For four minutes, make a list of everything that *makes you happy*. List anything that comes to mind by *speedwriting*. This means you write as fast as you can without stopping. Include things both large and small. Don't judge your answers. The idea here is to allow internal "stuff" to surface.

4. When the timer goes off, stop writing immediately. Make a note of how you feel. Often, making the list will actually change your body chemistry. Many people have a feeling of lightness or exhilaration after speedwriting their list. Some feel relaxed and others may experience sadness.

At this point, it doesn't matter what you've put on your list; what's important is experiencing the process of identification and how it makes you feel. Like Peter's fresh apricots, all kinds of surprising entries may appear on your list.

5. Study your list. Ask yourself:

How do I feel about what I've written? Surprised? Frustrated?

Was it difficult for me to come up with things? Did I "freeze up" as I wrote?

How much of the list reflects who I really am? How much reflects what I've been told to enjoy or desire?

You can use identification during your day, whenever you're faced with a decision. It can become your guide to making effective decisions that are right for you. You might ask, "What direction/items/choices will make me happiest at this moment?"

For most of us, simply thinking about what makes us happy makes us feel good. Identification feels good when we feel capable of implementing our vision of happiness. We feel competent and strong.

But what if your Dream List leaves you feeling unhappy?

Some of us feel unhappy when we envision something that is beyond our reach—something we love or want that we think we can't have. It's like window shopping with no possibility of buying.

If making a Dream List has left you with unhappy feelings, don't be discouraged. The next chapters titled "Centrality" and "Recasting" will deal with implementing your list and with the roadblocks to happiness.

Note: Be sure to keep your list; you'll need it again in Chapter 4.

Is Happiness Superficial and Self-Indulgent?

The apparent simplicity of the identification exercise belies its life-transforming potential. Margaret, a participant in one of our workshops, had always considered the desire to be happy as superficial and self-indulgent. A therapist and author, she thought of herself as a woman of depth who'd spent her life trying to "make a contribution," primarily through her work in the community. Personal happiness seemed like a silly objective. Her experiences in the workshop changed her mind:

> At first the question "What makes me happy?" sounded shallow. When I created my Dream List in the workshop, I judged myself for how simple and insignificant things like "walks on the beach" and "long bubble baths" were, compared to more important things, like service and duty.
>
> But as the workshop progressed, the question of happiness began to move me. I saw how I could really improve the quality of my life by indulging myself in these small ways. I felt I didn't need to accept my life the way it was. It was as though I was seduced by the power to make myself happy. If I could be happy in these small ways, why couldn't I make myself happy in large ways? From the beginning the process of identification had a profound effect on my whole life.
>
> I believe more than ever about giving back to the community. But now I also believe that I can build happiness into my life. When I do, I'm more energized and effective and less stressed. I'm nurturing myself as I nurture the community.

Margaret has overcome her most significant obstacle—feeling that she didn't deserve to spend time on herself. She is more loving toward herself.

The power of seemingly trivial items on your Dream List may amaze you, as it did Margaret. Along with walks on the beach and bubble baths, Margaret also listed fresh flowers as one of the small pleasures that brought her true happiness. Several weeks after the workshop Margaret laughingly invited us to her home, where we found room after room in bloom.

> I feel so happy when I see those flowers. Making the list was a great success. I carry my note pad with me everywhere. I feel joy moving through me as I write. My purse is full of scrap paper with scribbles.

These scribbles are the true leanings of my heart. I used to think that joy was momentary and fleeting—the bluebird of happiness flying in and out of my life. But now I see that happiness is a steady state inside me and that it's always there waiting for me, no matter what is happening in my life.

The process of identification can happen all day long. What will make us happiest at this moment? Listening to jazz on the Walkman, planning a dinner party, envisioning a trip to Hawaii.

Identification has a rich side effect, as well. As we delve into our psyches we broaden our awareness of our entire emotional palette. We make contact with the full range of our emotional, intellectual and material needs.

I'd rather have roses on my table than diamonds on my neck.

Emma Goldman

Happiness in the Long Term

Identification gives us insight—that is, sight into ourselves. It brings out our most emotionally healthy choices. By strengthening our insight into what is best for us, it supports our efforts to avoid self-destructive urges.

Bonnie and Robert

Walking home from her Saturday morning watercolor class on the first sunny day of spring, Bonnie glowed at the thought of the long, lazy afternoon ahead with Robert, her live-in boyfriend of three years. She thought about how nice it would be for the two of them to stroll around town, browse through the shops, maybe stop for coffee—all the things they looked forward to doing now that the long Ann Arbor winter was over.

Bonnie was a genuinely happy person who was thrilled to be with a gentle and caring man after a string of unsatisfying relationships. But Bonnie's past had left her with some residual insecurities and doubts about her chances of having a long-term relationship.

Her insecurity kicked in when she got home and found not Robert, but an uncharacteristically terse note: "Went to work, see you later." The note made Bonnie uneasy; she saw it as a sign that Robert was pulling away. An all-too-familiar feeling in the pit of Bonnie's stomach told her that their relationship might be in jeopardy. What was going on at work? Had something changed in their relationship?

Bonnie knew that Robert was uncomfortable talking about anything negative. And lately, Robert didn't want to talk about work. From the brusque tone of the note, she guessed it would be hours before he came home. It would be a long wait.

I asked myself what I should do in the meantime. Frankly, my first thought was to pour myself a glass of wine and watch TV. That might calm me down and divert my attention until he got home. Next, I thought I'd spend the afternoon on the phone with my friends, talking about Robert and what he was up to. Maybe I'd feel better about the situation, especially if I could get their support.

I fought the urge to do either of these things. A drink might make me feel better, but it would also dull my ability to talk with Robert. And talking to friends might really get my suspicions running wild. Would they help me and make me feel happier? Clearly, the answer was no.

What was making me tense was the fear that my relationship with Robert was going to end. I started to look for other ways I could control my fear. What could I do that would make me feel good about myself?

Bonnie's most self-affirming choice was simple—to go for a run. As basic as the choice was, it would make her feel happier and give her a greater sense of self-worth. After a long jog she thought she'd be better equipped to handle any eventuality with Robert.

This is a clear example of the interplay between mind and body. Bonnie's best emotional decision was the physically healthiest decision. Taking care of her body was the best way to clear her mind. What Bonnie experiences as happiness is both physical and psychological. Her mind and body are part of a single complex system.

As it turned out, Robert came home to a concerned, loving woman whose intention was to deal proactively with the issues. Bonnie's openness and nondefensiveness made Robert feel safe. He found in Bonnie an ally in solving what turned out to be looming business issues.

See the false as false,
The true as true.
Look into your heart,
Follow your nature.

The Dhammapada

"What Will Make You Happy, Dear?"

Most of us want our spouses to be happy. Irv was no exception.

He and Maryann had been married for ten years—and he loved her dearly. This was a late-in-life second marriage for both of them. Irv's greatest desire was that Maryann be happy, because when she was happy, he was happy.

From the outside looking in, Irv seemed to be an ideal mate. When it came time to buy a new house, make plans for the weekend, or even pick a movie to see, Irv sought out Maryann's opinions and made sure her desires were met. At other times, when there was little information to go on, he would second-guess what she wanted, believing this proved his devotion to her. But, despite his efforts, Maryann was frustrated.

Both Irv and Maryann attended one of our workshops. When it came time to create his Dream List, Irv got right to work. He was able to make a lengthy list, and when he compared his list with Maryann's, they were nearly identical.

> We looked at one another and knew what had happened: Everything on my list was something Maryann loved. Here was our problem staring me in the face. I couldn't distinguish between what I needed for myself, and what she needed.
>
> I had always assumed that it didn't really matter to me where we went or what we did or how we scheduled. All that mattered was making Maryann happy. But it seemed that she was always hostile. And the madder she got, the more I tried to please her.

Irv wasn't identifying from the heart, so Maryann found him distant and opaque. This stemmed from a childhood pattern Irv had carried into his adult relationships. He had always thought it was his obligation to make his mother happy, so it was natural he would relate to other women in the same way.

> Mother's desires were so many and so extreme that I became skillful at assessing her needs, but not my own. That's why when Maryann asked me what I wanted, I honestly didn't know.
>
> After the workshop I set out to discover my own needs, to be able to make my own Dream List. The hardest part was clearing my head of everyone else's ideas. Then I had to keep asking myself, "What do I really want? Me. Just me."
>
> Over the course of the next several days I focused all my attention and thoughts on uncovering things that really do make me happy. And when I was able to share those things with Maryann, I felt more genuine than I ever had before.

We met with Irv and Maryann several months after the workshop. What was the impact of his self-discovery? The real surprise was that Maryann loved the new Irv. She didn't want to be catered to. She didn't want a compliant husband—a cardboard cut-out figure. She wanted to know the real Irv. By sharing his honest feelings with her, he was infusing new energy into the relationship, and she felt much closer to him.

Knowing others is wisdom,
knowing yourself is Enlightenment.

Lao Tzu

Moving Through Tragedy

In Chapter 2 we met Jerry, who exhibited an extraordinary degree of accountability when his son, Steven, was killed by a truck in rural Alabama. You may have wondered what Jerry did, specifically, to be so accountable? He used identification.

Of course, for all of us, identification is easiest during joyful periods and hardest during painful periods. Identifying what will make us happier at a time when we're drowning in sorrow may even seem impossible or inappropriate. Even though it may seem unusual, Jerry's ability to identify what would make him happiest during the trauma allowed him to keep his perspective and not descend into despondency.

> *There is very little I remember about the first days after Steven's death. I do know that when I began my healing process, I kept saying to myself that my greatest responsibility was to make decisions that would allow me and my wife to feel happy again.*
>
> *So many decisions had to be made at a time when my ability to make sound judgments was impaired. Looking for the route that would prove the happiest in the long run was the clearest*

guide I had. The funeral, the wake, the flow of visitors all required decisions. And I directed each decision toward feeling better, toward clearing the fog of despair instead of losing myself in it.

As I struggled through each day, I could feel some deep sense of my old self waiting to break through.

As a counterbalance to his sadness, identification promised Jerry the possibility of happier times. Someday. Jerry's decisions left him feeling more oriented—if not happier—than he would have felt had he not used the identification process.

Eventually I realized that I had laid the groundwork for moving ahead. Steven's death had certainly become part of my fabric, but I was also aware of the terrible possibility that his death could overwhelm my life—that the emotional pain would pervade my identity. I did have one momentous choice to make. I could either choose to live the rest of my life as an unhappy person or a happy person. I owed it to myself and to Steven to be happy. I was clear on my route.

If people are happy during a terrible crisis, we think of them as sociopaths at worst, and disconnected from reality at best. But Jerry's story is different—it is a testament to the *possibility of eventual happiness*, even after a tragedy.

Being "In the Mush"

Obviously, when something this horrible happens we can't just push a button to make it all better. Clearly, it has taken time for Jerry to move from despair back to a happy life. But, as difficult as it was, the dark period after losing Steven was critical for healing. During this time, it was his continued use of the identification process that enabled him to re-establish his priorities, feelings, values and viewpoints—to become the person he is today.

For many years we have honored that "in-between" stage of growth and healing in our weekly men's group. Our metaphor for this kind of change is the metamorphosis of a caterpillar to chrysalis to butterfly.

If you were to cut open a chrysalis as the butterfly develops, you might expect to find a partly formed butterfly inside. But this isn't the case. Inside is an unrecognizable "mush"—the gray protoplasm that will reconstruct itself and ultimately emerge as a butterfly. This ugly, sticky stuff has all the elements necessary to create great beauty. It just takes time.

We need to decide that it's OK for us to be in this unsure, uncomfortable place. In fact, most of the time it's exactly where we need to be. Just as "being in the mush" was a crucial step for Jerry, it is also a necessary period of growth in the achievement of any significant, life-altering change.

Fortunately, a great deal of growth comes from nontraumatic situations. Tony reached a point in his life when he needed to make a momentous change. And he had the courage to step into the mush.

We have what we seek. It is there all the time, and if we give it time, it will make itself known to us.

Thomas Merton

Tony's Dream List

In the late 1980s, Tony was on top of the world. As chief financial officer of a mid-sized computer company in Silicon Valley, he thrived on the fast pace of this high-tech financial environment, working ten-hour days and loving every minute of it. In the early 1990s, a glut of software developers saturated the market, and times got tough for Tony's company.

In a burst of panic, the president of the firm pulled Tony aside and "suggested" that he manipulate the company's financial reports to portray a more favorable picture. Although the request was not illegal, Tony felt the integrity of the company was being eroded. Not only did he feel uncomfortable about the president's request, he started to feel disheartened about the way employees were being treated.

He wasn't having fun anymore. Tony now dreaded getting out of bed in the morning. Once a source of joy, his job was now the source of uneasiness and depression. What would he want to do if he weren't concerned about the money? If he could craft his perfect day, what would it look like?

> *In my fantasy world, it came down to three things. I wanted to teach. Training had always been my favorite part of the job. I wanted to have the time to help other people—to be actively involved in a nonprofit organization. But, most of all, I wanted to have time to do things for myself, like outings with the family, golf, exercise and cooking up my mother's Italian recipes.*

Could this dream become a reality? What would he have to give up? Tony wasn't sure, but he noticed that he felt better just having identified what he really wanted to do. At the same time the task ahead was daunting.

Is it possible for him to make the things that are important to his happiness central to his life? As we'll see in the next chapter, "centrality" is the next step in achieving lasting contentment.

Many men go fishing all of their lives without knowing that it is not fish they are after.

Henry David Thoreau

Accountability → Identification →

Intention

Centrality

Centrality

I didn't pay any attention when everyone told me I should get a real job. I love performing. I feel it's a gift. I never wanted to do anything else, even when I was a kid. And I did it!

Paula Gaffin, Broadway chorus dancer

A person will be called to account on judgment day for every permissible thing that he might have enjoyed but did not.

Jerusalem Talmud, tractate Kiddushin, chapter 4, paragraph 12

Centrality is happy people's nonnegotiable choice to pursue the greatest passions of their minds and hearts. In other words, they make central to the lives that which brings them the greatest joy. This is what energizes them. And it's what integrates them into their world.

There's a wisdom and fierceness to living centralities. It's actualizing our Dream Lists, insisting that we don't overlook ourselves as life passes by. It's persisting in living our days to the fullest, spending them doing the things we love, regardless of the many pressures on us to do otherwise. When we centralize, we support our own growth, even if that growth requires some impressive action. We are like the mother eagle who nurtures her fledglings by pushing them out of the nest so they will develop into the magnificent creatures they have the potential to become.

Centralities are an expression of who we are as authentic individuals. They're what make us feel most vital and alive. And in their diversity, they celebrate the variety of human experience. Whether it's spending time with grandchildren or rock climbing, living our centralities makes our individual path unique, exciting and well worth following.

What stops us from taking this path? There are many reasons we find it hard to centralize. Some of us feel trapped by responsibilities—both financial and emotional. We have children to raise, bills to pay, work to do. As much as we'd like to act on our Dream List, we don't see it as a viable choice, at least not right now. But we need to consider that if we don't do the things we love, we cannot expect to be fully happy.

So how do we do it? Centralizing may seem difficult, but it can be as easy as choosing one item each day from your Dream List. Even pushing ourselves to do little things, like cooking dinner with our spouses or filling the house with cut flowers, can add richness to our lives. We forget how meaningful simple pleasures can be.

Even under the most difficult circumstances, happy people find a way to centralize. Every extremely happy person we encountered managed in some way to build a life around his or her passions. Doing so requires ingenuity and creativity, and in this chapter we'll give you portraits of happy people who have made changes in order to be happy.

I finally figured out the only reason to be alive is to enjoy it.

Rita Mae Brown

Tony Centralizes His Dream List

Whether you begin to cook dinner more often with your spouse or finally sign up for that class in flower arranging, centralizing is about honoring your internal values, needs and interests. It may also involve actualizing your need for major life changes. This often means debunking the social expectations and material mandates that frequently rule your life.

Tony, the financial officer we met in Chapter 3, began his story when the president of his company asked him to alter financial records. This prompted him to identify what he wanted to do with his life. But could he realistically achieve the things on his Dream List? Tony wanted to teach, to be involved in helping others and to have more time to spend with his family. But he was afraid. If he acted on that list he might lose too much.

The most apparent loss was the security of a well-paid job with a guaranteed salary and benefits package. He would be seen differently in the community. He might lose friendships at work, a structured schedule and a stable place to go every day.

But Tony also considered what he would gain, most notably, a chance to be happy with himself again.

I spent some sleepless nights agonizing over the decision to leave the job. My last and most difficult hurdle was to let go of my insecurities.

The reality is, the world is changing so fast, I don't believe there's such a thing as job security anymore. So if my job is going to change anyway, why not do what makes me happiest. At least that way I'll have control over where I'm headed.

I stopped worrying about whether or not I was going to be successful. I decided I'd rather be a "failure" doing the things I love than a "success" in a situation that makes me unhappy.

One morning I took a leap of faith. For years everyone had trusted my judgment. So I finally decided to trust myself.

Tony began to put the centralization process in motion. His first undertaking was to teach a night class at a nearby university. Over the course of the semester, Tony discussed the unethical demands that had been made on him with the head of the university's Finance Department. As a result, they created a new course entitled "Business Ethics."

I figured if I couldn't fight the battle at the corporate level, I could at least influence the next generation of businesspeople. My life was already changing for the better.

As a teacher, Tony was a natural; the university asked him to teach a full schedule of classes for the following semester. He took the plunge, finally quitting his corporate job to become a full-time college instructor.

Tony was already a member of a nonprofit organization dedicated to helping the disadvantaged in the community. The part-time position of financial officer for the organization became available. It didn't pay much, but he loved the work so he took the job. Even with both jobs, he made only 70 percent of his previous income.

The money was secondary. I had opportunities to earn more. In fact, my old company offered me some consulting work. But I didn't want to put myself in that environment again. Besides, that commitment would have gotten in the way of what I really wanted to do.

Now I play golf twice a week. On Sunday evenings, my wife and I cook gourmet Italian meals. We make a mean risotto and enough spinach ravioli and fresh gnocchi to last us the whole week.

Acting on his Dream List was like setting off a line of dominoes; each passion led naturally to the next. As Tony traveled to and from the university, he noticed a number of impoverished migrant workers in the rural areas of the county. So with a friend, he now heads up a volunteer organization that delivers sandwiches to day laborers. The organization not only provides food to needy people, it gives dozens of Tony's friends and neighbors a way to contribute to their community. Every morning a group of people arrives at Tony's house, where his kitchen has been converted into a bustling box-lunch assembly line.

I love my new life. Am I any less busy than before? No. Am I happier? Oh yes! I don't feel like I'm in that rat race anymore. Every morning I get up excited by the prospect of the variety the day will bring. I've got my dream life. I wouldn't change a thing.

The trouble with being in the rat race is that
even if you win, you're still a rat.

Lily Tomlin

Tony is an unusual man who has crafted an unusual professional existence for himself. But happy people with more conventional jobs also create surprising and interesting lives outside of their occupations.

Trudi, a car-rental clerk in Tulsa, uses her free time to be a legislative advocate for preschool children. Millie finally retired at age eighty-nine after working for decades as a secretary in a Manhattan theatrical agency—a job she loved—and now continues to attend theater performances three or four times each week. And Leah, a safety engineer for a major chemical company, loves swimming and politics. At the time of our interview she was moderating a debate on national politics for the League of Women Voters before leaving for Hawaii to compete in a swimming marathon.

Centralities are the focal points in the lives of happy adults. But many of their centralities began to form in childhood.

A Lifelong Love of Nature

Jean-Claude is a scientist for a large international agency. He naturally created his own Dream List as a child in Quebec and has never considered living without it.

> *The things I most love have colored my entire life. As a child, the village priest took me and the other kids through the meadows to bless the crops. Each spring, we wandered through a countryside rich with apple orchards and wildflowers. I fell in love with nature then—and this love has stayed with me for fifty years.*

As a university student Jean-Claude was drawn to water sciences and engineering. This led him directly to a life as a satellite scientist. He studies the earth's entire ecology from the skies— particularly water resources and rain forests.

> *I have a philosophy I live by. When I focus on what I love, I get what I love. And that's exactly what I do. I pour all my energy into studying the environment, and that way I have no time left over for negative things like cynicism and criticism. This has propelled me in a positive direction and distinguished me among my colleagues. Everyone knows how passionate I am about what I do. This has led to all kinds of job opportunities and travel possibilities.*

I have never considered going into another field. I've walked through the Mongolian steppes and the Southeast Asian Golden Triangle. I've been in all the major rain forests and watched with fascination as massive fires burned in Siberia. I feel stimulated every day. I live and breathe to study the environment.

Unlike Jean-Claude, many of us don't identify our passions—or act on them—until we are adults. What stops us? Perhaps we don't have Jean-Claude's childhood insights. Perhaps we don't have the financial resources to live our dreams. But is money really the issue?

Cash Versus Centrality

On one hand, we believe that if we have money, it's a lot easier to be happy. And why not? We could afford to do anything we want.

On the other hand, our mothers always said, "Money doesn't buy happiness."

Who's right?

Mom is.

Studies of lottery winners show that one year after winning the jackpot, these new millionaires are no happier than they were before. In fact, many are *less* happy.

Still, most of us say, "If I won the lottery, I know *I'd* be happier. Is there something wrong with these people?"

No, there's nothing wrong with them. Money's reputation is overblown. It doesn't nurture us or feed our souls. And people with a great deal of money have far more to lose when they set out to make their Dream Lists a reality. Often they're trapped by a world of overwhelming material commitments that they must support.

While doing our research we had a dramatic experience that proves this point. While in Los Angeles, we did back-to-back interviews with two extremely happy people—Regina, a society matron living in an enormous mansion, and Elena, a housemaid living in the *barrio,* just above the poverty line. In extensive interviews with the two women we heard exactly the same stories. Not the same facts, but the identical set of behaviors—the nine choices of happy people. With regard to centralities, the only difference between the two was that one set was more expensive than the other.

Many of us know wealthy people who are miserable. We've also heard of people who have given up lucrative jobs to live joyful lives. Lawyers have become teachers; business executives have become small business owners. They are just discovering what happy people already know: In order for us to live our passions, creativity and problem-solving—not money—are the keys.

Often people attempt to live their lives backwards: they try to have more things, or more money, in order to do more of what they want so that they will be happier. The way it actually works is the reverse. You must first be who you really are, then, do what you need to do, in order to have what you want.

Margaret Young

Giving Up Money, Getting Happy

Barbara married Paul in the early 1980s, just as he became a writer-producer on several of the hottest TV sitcoms. Together they lived the Hollywood life to the hilt: his-and-her Porsches, parties with celebrities, invitations to the Emmy Awards. To the same extent that Paul was a thoughtful and quiet type, Barbara was an intense, vivacious and determined woman.

When they bought their fifteen-room Brentwood estate, Barbara was thrilled. She set out with a vengeance to decorate her dream home with a team of designers, hand-picking each tile and mulling over every paint chip.

I was smart enough to know that nothing made me happier than using my own creativity. It turned out that I was right about creativity, but wrong in the way I used it.

I managed to turn our house into a showcase. It was gorgeous! But the day we finished the project, I had a sinking feeling in my stomach. I found myself wondering, "What else can I buy?" So, I kept on shopping . . . and shopping . . . and shopping. The excitement of each new purchase lasted about two days, and then I needed another "fix." It was a trap. No matter how much buying I did, I was never really satisfied.

Money was my downfall. Because I didn't have to work, there were a lot of days I just stayed home. My life felt flat.

All of our friends were rich. Money and what it could buy became the substance of our lives. We didn't do anything that was productive—it was all about showing off the cash, talking about the latest resort or newest, most fabulous restaurant in town.

Paul wasn't happy either. Sometimes he would be without a show for months and be desperate to sign a new contract. To maintain our lifestyle Paul needed to generate a huge amount of cash. And each month we spent every dime he made.

We "had it all," but at the same time we had nothing. And that "nothing" was costing us dearly. We weren't happy. I knew we had to do something.

A frustrated and pressured Paul agreed. They began to explore their centralities. Barbara kept thinking about the word *creativity,* understanding now that it was not about buying, but about self-expression.

I remembered back to my high school days. I had been dyslexic, so academic subjects that required reading were a struggle for me. But I was a star student in art, particularly in sculpting.

After graduation, I landed a great job in set design. In fact,
before I married Paul my career had been really fulfilling.

After months of self-examination, Barbara and Paul knew they
had both turned their backs on dreams that they had assumed
wouldn't generate much income. Barbara wanted to sculpt. Paul had
always wanted to write freelance on his own terms. In order to do
what they really loved, they would have to give up Paul's extraordinary earning potential, sell the house at a loss and say good-bye to
Hollywood.

A decade ago they walked away from a life of which most people can only dream.

I'd wake up in the middle of the night and think, Are we crazy?
Will we live to regret this? But I knew better. There was no way I
was going to end up as a regretful old lady looking back on my
life, knowing I'd never been really happy. The image of that old
crone gave me the guts to do it.

To do it right, I was prepared to risk everything we had. I
wanted to move to Italy. I knew it was the best place in the world
to learn my craft. It had the best artisans and the best materials.
It also had the best marble quarries.

We took off for Italy with four large suitcases and a key to the
storage locker that held a few of our favorite mementos. We
didn't speak Italian, and we didn't know anyone in Italy. There
were so many unknowns, but I had enough faith in myself to
give it a shot.

Today, ten years later, the woman at work in Tuscany is a very
different person from the Hollywood Barbara. In her studio, surrounded by the deafening noise from her electric sculpting tools and
coated in white marble dust, Barbara sculpts her fine pieces in the
same Carrara marble Michelangelo once used. Barbara also serves as
an art gallery associate and teaches modern sculpting techniques.

My life is now gritty, dusty and physically exhausting. I'm down in the studio at seven and fall into bed at ten. I'm certainly no longer the Hollywood princess. I live in four rooms, drive a tiny Fiat, do my own laundry. I've created my perfect life in a culture I love, with people I love. I get to use all my best talents. And I love it.

When we visited Barbara, she jostled us and two of our children over back roads for a tour of the quarries and treated us to antipasto and wine in a tiny trattoria. Afterward, we were given a lesson in sculpting technique. Barbara handed each of us a chunk of marble and a set of old-fashioned chisels. At that moment we could see her excitement, which confirmed beyond any words her feeling of joy.

The week before our visit, Barbara had been awarded first prize in an international art competition. Offers to travel and meet with art representatives and buyers from around the world flooded in. But she demurred.

What makes me happy? Working in the studio, feeling the tools in my hands, talking to the artisans, helping customers in the gallery. What doesn't work for me? Notoriety, jet-setting, publicity, money. I'll never be sucked back into that world again. I'm going to do the things that make me happy; and I'm going to turn down offers that won't make me happy.

And what about Paul? He's taken his lead from Barbara. Because he doesn't write in Italian, his skills are most saleable in English-speaking countries. From the tiled roof garden of their small apartment, he sends articles and TV scripts to London and New York via E-mail.

Faith in one's self . . . is the best and safest course.

Michelangelo

Keisha's Garden

Unlike Barbara and Paul, Keisha is poor. She was raised by her grandmother in the bayou country of Louisiana in a modest wood house lifted up on pilings along the Pearl River. With great pride Grammy and Keisha tended the lush garden every day after school. They looked forward to full days of gardening during summer vacation. Together they produced zinnias, nasturtiums and strawberries.

Keisha loved every part of the growing cycle—planting the seeds, watering them each night and watching them sprout into mature plants.

When Keisha was fourteen, Grammy died suddenly of a stroke. The house was sold and she was sent to San Francisco to live with her aunt and uncle. Life changed; she found herself in public housing, where there were no gardens to tend and no lazy afternoons playing along the river. It felt to Keisha that her happiness had vanished overnight.

High school was rough. Keisha was used to a more gentle existence. The neighborhood was unsafe, the kids were unruly, and the surroundings were devoid of color and beauty.

> I was always daydreaming about Louisiana—working in my garden, feeling the soil, cutting back the flowers, growing our own vegetables and fruits.
>
> After high school most of my friends took jobs as cashiers and store clerks. But not me. I looked in the phone book and found three garden nurseries. I hopped on the bus to find a job.
>
> I'd never applied for a job before, and I'd never been to a nursery. Nobody had a job for me. But just walking down the rows of plants made me feel like I was back home. I knew in my heart I belonged here.

She kept going back every week for two months. Finally her persistence paid off when she landed a job as a groundskeeper's assistant.

Five years later she's still working as the beloved employee of a family-run nursery.

Recently Keisha purchased her first house, a tiny cottage in a run-down neighborhood. But this cottage came with something very important, a twenty-by-twenty-foot plot of land in front of the house.

Driving down the street, it's hard to miss Keisha's house. Her garden is a colorful oasis in an otherwise bleak and gray neighborhood, a wall-to-wall carpet of yellow, orange and purple. Tomatoes and zucchini grow among the hollyhocks, zinnias and gladiolus.

> *I did this all on fifty dollars' worth of seed and bulbs. I feel so happy when I'm sitting in the garden. It reminds me of home. I have so much here. What I don't need I give away.*

Beloved by her neighbors for her generous bouquets, Keisha is known throughout the community as "the garden lady." This notoriety brought about a phone call from a local elementary-school principal. Keisha now visits classrooms and teaches inner-city school kids how to plant their own gardens with limited land and money.

Keisha's life has come full circle, sharing with a new generation what her grandmother shared with her.

Regardless of where they come from—Brentwood or the projects—Barbara, Paul and Keisha have something precious in common: They are all doing what makes them happiest.

You don't need money to centralize. You don't have to win the lottery to do what you love. It's about following your heart. But acting on your Dream List requires some preliminary steps: the intention to be happy, the determination, flexibility and willingness to take risks that come from personal accountability, and the self-knowledge that comes from the identification process.

Insecurity, Instability and Centrality

You might be thinking all of this is great for these people. Tony's children are grown and he has paid his mortgage. Barbara and Paul started off rich and weren't overburdened by debt when they left for Italy. Keisha had little to lose when she abandoned the projects to became a gardener.

You're different. Centralizing your greatest interests or passions would totally disrupt your life—you don't have the luxury of making these kinds of dramatic changes!

In fact, stability and security are important to most of us. We strive to create a secure, stable environment for ourselves and our families, and we naturally resist giving any of this up.

But what are we really giving up? Can we ever be truly secure?

Many events illustrate how quickly life can change. Would any of us have anticipated the waves of corporate downsizing that have put millions out of work? Did we anticipate the AIDS epidemic and its profound effect on our sexual mores and behavior? Not one major financial institution predicted that a crisis in the Thai currency would have a lasting impact on the major world economies.

Such unpredictable events affect thousands of people every day. Like it or not, change, instability and insecurity are a fundamental part of our world. If insecurity is a given, why not make ourselves happier by taking the risk of doing what we love?

By centralizing, happy people move through life with a degree of personal security and self-assertion. Paradoxically, by accepting life's inherent instability they become more secure than many of us.

Centralizing What Makes You Happy

In Chapter 3, you made a Dream List by speedwriting. In this exercise you will be referring to that list.

1. Review your Dream List from Chapter 3. Have you forgotten any items that belong there? Add anything else that makes you happy.

2. Make a check mark next to anything that you do regularly. These are things you are already centralizing.

3. Take a look at the items on the list that you don't currently centralize. If you did centralize them, you might be considerably more happy. Think about the following questions:

> As you look at all of these items, is there a theme?
>
> What are you failing to centralize in your personal life? Your professional life?
>
> What's stopping you?
>
> Can you easily integrate some of these things into your life?

Very often, major problems are stopping us from centralizing. If this is the case, don't despair. We'll show you how happy people break through major roadblocks to happiness in Chapter 5, "Recasting."

When Life Gets in Our Way

We have found that parenting and health problems are among the most commonly stated reasons people feel they can't act on their

Dream Lists. This is not a surprise because both these issues are largely intractable. We'd have to wait a long time for the kids to grow up or, in the case of illness, for medical miracles.

We're also questioned about people living in different political cultures. Do people have the choice to be happy in totalitarian societies?

The following stories are about three remarkable women: a new mother and corporate manager, a retired teacher who contends with chronic illness, and a courageous non-conformist as she looks back over the last fifty years of her life in a communist regime.

Married, with Children, and Working, Too

At our happiness workshops we frequently hear from women who are juggling family lives and careers: "I am so exhausted at the end of the day that I just don't have the time or energy to do anything other than what I *have* to do. How can I centralize when there's no time left for me?"

Gillian, thirty-three, understands all too well. She is one of the extremely happy people whom we knew before our research began. She has an incredible ability to get things done with humor and style. Everyone loves her. But even Gil reached a point in her life when she felt her happiness slip away. In her comfortable home in Seattle, Washington, she told us how she regained her happiness when the challenges in her life began to overwhelm her.

Gillian worked hard to put her husband, Scott, through law school. On the day Scott graduated, she gave birth to their first child. Gillian loved being a new mother, and she was thrilled when Scott got his first job, thinking she might have more time to do things just for herself.

But it didn't turn out that way. Her life grew more hectic. Gillian returned to work in a new, demanding managerial job. The baby was colicky and Scott was away from home a lot, putting in the extra hours required of a first-year lawyer.

Although I loved my family and my work, I felt that I was losing myself. I was drowning in a flood of demands. My daily schedule was actually determined by everybody else's schedule. I was giving all day: at home I was a nurturing mother and supportive wife; and, at work, I coached the staff and serviced customers. I thought to myself, "Hey, who's going to do any of these things for me?" My answer was obvious: ME! I set out to find myself again.

Gillian came up with a plan that would satisfy all her needs. It would provide time alone, relief from the pressure, a feeling of physical well-being and a feeling of accomplishment. The solution: to fulfill a dream by competing in a mini-triathlon—a half-mile swim, twelve-mile bike ride, and three-mile run all combined into one event.

It was a real stretch for me but I stayed committed. The training was just for me. Since the race happened to be on my birthday, I considered it a gift to myself.

Implementing my plan was not so easy. My first step was to sit down with Scott and be very honest with him about how important this was to me. I remember looking him right in the eye and saying, "Scott, I have to do this for myself." He understood and we collaborated on a plan. He agreed to fix the baby's breakfast and get him to day care so I could go to the track before work.

The second step was to let go of the guilt. My mother exploded when I told her my plan. "Oh Gillian, are you nuts? With all you have to do at work and with the baby." I had to silence the little voice in my head that said, "If you're a good person, you'll have dinner on the table for the baby and Scott. . . . The baby is your first priority. . . . You have no right to do something for yourself." Believe me, getting rid of the guilt was the hardest part.

Gillian began her training by getting up every morning and running three miles. She took a long bike ride after work each day and swam twice a week. Her training paid off; she won her division in the triathlon.

> It's true that I had to lower my standards in the housekeeping and babysitting departments. But this was completely overshadowed by the end results. I had a terrific sense of personal accomplishment, and this led to some unanticipated benefits. First, Scott developed a real attachment to the baby that came from having to be the primary caregiver for a few months. Second, I was really able to focus better at work. I felt healthier— not nearly as nervous and preoccupied. Third, I think the baby has benefited the most. Deep down I think I resented the constraints he put on me. By allowing some time for myself, I regained control over my own life. I don't have to keep running triathlons to know that I can take some time to do things just for myself.

Centralizing requires having enough self-worth to withstand pressures—from our loved ones, our bosses and from our own internal voices. If we wait for unanimous support, it will never come. At any given time, some people will be supportive, others will be critical. Making everyone around us happy is an impossible task. It is enough to make ourselves happy.

We can always justify why it's impossible, right now, to take care of ourselves. But if we wait for the perfect time, we will wait forever. We need to take care of ourselves all the time.

If you always do what interests you,
then at least one person is pleased.

Katharine Hepburn's mother

Never Giving Up

Lena was diagnosed with a rare bone disease in 1973. At the time she was a successful fifty-year-old elementary school teacher who loved her work. The news was devastating.

> *My work was my life. Every part of my day was filled with things I loved—the children and the other teachers were a perfect world for me. I felt intellectually stimulated and embraced by the educational community. Up to that point, my life was wonderful.*
>
> *The doctors told me to prepare for an early retirement. I could expect to be in extreme pain and totally disabled within a few years, and I'd have to give up teaching.*

With the support of her husband, Jack, Lena began an endless round of second and third and fourth opinions, all to no avail. The best doctors in the country agreed that Lena faced a shortened life-span, disability and pain. There was nothing medicine could do, and nothing Lena could do. But this was a prognosis Lena would not accept.

> *The doctors were wrong. Of course there was something I could do—there is always something I can do!*
>
> *I did some research and confirmed the fact that this illness simply has no cure. So I accepted the disease as a given in my life. What was, was. I thought to myself, "Okay, if I'm going to be sick, how can I keep doing what I want to do?"*
>
> *I would certainly lose my ability to walk. I would certainly be in pain. Givens. But I could be crippled and in pain at home, in bed, missing out on life. Or I could be crippled and in pain at work—being stimulated by life. The choice was obvious.*

Lena continued to work. As the illness progressed, so did she. She changed from an ambulatory teacher with a new diagnosis to a teacher on crutches, and finally, to a teacher in a wheelchair. Her aspirin-based painkillers gave way to ibuprofen and then high-tech medications and acupuncture.

> *It became more difficult for me to move around, but I became a better teacher than I'd ever been before. I think I provided a wonderful learning experience for my students. I taught them a great deal about disabilities and tolerance. Rather than recoiling from a crippled teacher, they became very protective of me, taking turns pushing my wheelchair. Because we had an environment of love and respect, I had very few disciplinary problems in my classroom.*
>
> *My real goal, though, was to continue doing what I loved. I far exceeded the projections of the doctors. I was able to work for almost fifteen years longer than they predicted. Now that I can't work, I'm doing other things I love. Each morning before I get out of bed I make a mental list of my plans.*
>
> *Almost every day I write poetry. I do mailings for political causes. I read and I do art projects with my grandchildren. Jack and I take long car trips. I can't imagine a richer life.*
>
> *I don't mean to make it sound easy. The pain is a reality that I have to deal with during every waking hour. It can be horrible. But I know that it would be worse if I give up what I love and spend all my time nursing myself.*

Lena lives her Dream List in spite of a body in physical revolt. But what happens to happy people when the political world revolts and ultimately makes living their dreams an act of treason?

If one advances confidently in the direction of his dreams and endeavors to live the life which he has imagined, he will meet with a success unexpected in common hours.

Henry David Thoreau

Looking Back

Most of us don't live in totalitarian countries where our lives are rigidly structured from the outside. Our government doesn't stop us from doing what we love. Others are not so lucky.

We were referred to seventy-six-year-old Kati by a physical therapist we know, who was once Kati's student and claims she is the most fearlessly happy person she knows. Kati has lived her entire life in an Eastern European capital. Through a translator, she told us her fascinating story of sheer perseverance and fortitude.

My life has been a series of doing what I love in the moment, regardless of the obstacles. Movement and dance, even talking about movement and dance—what we're doing right now—is something I love.

In the late 1930s Kati was a successful professional dancer appearing on avant-garde stages throughout Europe. During the Nazi occupation she feared that her Jewish heritage would mark her for "relocation," so she hid in the cellar of a bakery. In 1945, she emerged, stumbling into the post-war wreckage of Eastern Europe. Her fiancé had been killed in the camps, and her family members had all disappeared.

Further, the confluence of economic depression, Russian occupation and the newly installed communist regime made a career in modern dance virtually impossible. The government not only failed to support the experimental arts, but actively damned them. Anyone involved in these art forms was considered an enemy of the state and could suffer persecution.

I was just so happy to have survived that I optimistically started a school of "movement technique." I thought I'd get away with it if I didn't call it "dance."

The school was successful for two years until it was shut down by the regime in 1948. After it was barricaded, Kati began to teach movement and dance independently even though modern dance was not recognized as an employment category by the state. As an independent worker, this made her ineligible for social benefits.

During these years Kati developed an entire system of movement—what we would now call a "holistic" approach to body movement—that became well known in the fields of physical therapy and kinesiology. She was widely recognized in the underground arts world for her work.

In the early 1950s, Kati was approached by a well-known coach of the Olympic gymnastics team. At the time, music was just being introduced into the floor routines in women's gymnastics. Since dance had been discouraged by the government, the coach was desperate to find someone who could create dance routines. Ultimately Kati became the unofficial lead choreographer for the national team, which went on to win medals in both the Olympic and World Championship competitions.

> *I was neither invited to attend the Games nor recognized by the government for my work. The only recognition I received was a single red rose from one of the gymnasts' parents. I didn't care because I was so happy, so fulfilled. It didn't seem disappointing.*
>
> *I was so committed to what I loved that doing it provided all I ever wanted. Young people nowadays expect money and recognition, but these were not available to me and they were simply not important to my life.*

Kati continued to teach movement and kinesiology. Feeling that she needed a better understanding of human anatomy, she went back to school. Her education enabled her to create a movement and physical therapy handbook that became a standard guide. The book was published widely, but not under her name, and she received no credit or compensation for its success.

With the fall of the old regime, Kati has enjoyed new recognition. This past year she received an award from the president of the republic commemorating her achievement in dance and music. When we mentioned how exciting it must have been for her to be honored finally, she said:

> The ceremony was enjoyable, but this award means nothing to me. What really means something is how I feel about myself right now. I could have easily lived a safer and more comfortable life. But as I look back over almost eighty years, I don't think I'd like myself very well if I hadn't lived as I did.
>
> This past January my husband, the love of my life, died. Had I not taken risks, I would now be lonely and empty. Instead, I am filled with riches—a life of creativity, devoted and loving students and a deep interest in something that has affected many lives. I can look back at my life and truthfully say that I did what I love every single day.

How many of us can truthfully say that?

To be or not to be is not a question of compromise.
Either you be or you don't be.

Golda Meir

At this point, we've discussed four choices all happy people make. First, they have the active intention to be happy. Second, they are accountable to themselves and others, which leads them to make proactive choices. Third, they go through the process of identification, which serves to orient them to their needs and desires. Fourth, as we've seen in this chapter, they centralize those things that will truly work for them. They live their passions and follow their hearts.

Does this all sound too easy? What happens when things get in our way? How do happy people deal with life's inevitable problems and traumas?

Chapter 5

Accountability → Identification → Centrality → Recasting

Intention

Recasting

Without that saxophone in my mouth . . . I've learned to sing!

Maurice Washington, eighty-seven, professional
musician, on his inability to play his beloved
saxophone after a debilitating stroke

It's a kind of test, Mary, and it's the only kind that amounts to anything. When something rotten like this happens, then you have your choice. You start to really be alive, or you start to die. That's all.

James Agee,
A Death in the Family

Sometimes our hearts get broken. We lose the job. Someone we love dies. We can't always be in control over what happens, and we feel particularly vulnerable when large events shake our lives. We'd like to centralize our passions and have our dreams come true. But as much as we want to live happily, life's gauntlet gets in the way.

So how do we respond?

One way is to adopt the "get over it, get on with your life" strategy. Another way is to decide you'd rather stay upbeat and positive regardless of the severity of the situation. What entices us about these approaches is that they make it appear that we've gotten through the problem without having to feel the pain. But ultimately these approaches are forms of denial. And denial, unfortunately, fails to bring long-term happiness.

There's no way around the fact that life brings pain. It's part of the human experience. The question is "What do we do with that pain?" Happy people have an answer that is uniquely powerful and moving. One of the most extraordinary discoveries in our interviews is that happy people universally react to painful situations in the same way. We call it *recasting*. By recasting, they move through events that are otherwise debilitating, with an elegance and efficiency that is stunning.

How do they do it?

Recasting has two phases. First, happy people dive into negative feelings head on and experience them deeply. They listen to what their minds and bodies are telling them. They don't censor raw emotion, deny feelings or run from pain as many of us do in an attempt to "just go on." Rather, they honor their own emotional world by feeling it, even when avoidance would be easier.

Once they are fully engaged with their emotions they move into the second phase. They begin to transform their feelings with new reactions and insights. What lessons can they learn? What new meaning can they create for their lives? What opportunities for the future can they create from this experience?

Recasting ultimately lets happy people navigate through difficult times by raising the positive emotional value of an event. Even in the most traumatic situations, they search for the seeds of growth and insight.

The concept of recasting comes from the fire and heat of a steel mill. Imagine an emotional trauma that feels as if it's intractable—cast in steel. Its weight and hard edges are set. These traumas are often overwhelming events that are unchangeable—the loss of a job we've held for twenty years, a breakup with a lover or the death of a parent. Our emotions seem equally set: If the event is intractable, so are our feelings.

When we recast we put the event and our reactions into a psychological furnace and melt them down. Over time, we allow ourselves to feel the heat of negative emotions *and* forge a richer, deeper meaning from the trauma.

When we emerge, our experience has been changed. Its shape, look and feel are altered. Realistically, the raw material is the same metal, containing the same loss and hurt. But into the experience we may have infused new hope or spiritual value. Whether it takes days, months or years, new understandings or purpose may be shaped from a tragedy.

Underlying recasting is a powerful notion: We have the strength to master our reactions purposefully to even the most traumatic events, and, in so doing, transform ourselves. Therefore, we do not have to be held captive by sadness and loss. We can experience them fully and grow richer from having been in their shadow.

Recasting emerges as a potent tool that propels us toward emotional capability—a critical element as we choose to be happy.

In the depth of winter, I finally learned that
there was in me an invincible summer.

Albert Camus

Clara's House

Cleaning out the homes of loved ones after their death is an inevitable experience for most of us. Watching this kind of event unfold in the life of a happy person gives us insight into how recasting can help us live effectively through troubling yet predictable experiences.

Alan's story begins when his beloved aunt Clara, never married and childless, died unexpectedly at age sixty-nine. Alan had been her favorite nephew, and she had been his favorite aunt. Together he and his sister Deborah were faced with cleaning out her rambling two-story home—the same one in which they had spent many happy weekends as children. Clara had provided enrichment in their early lives, financing their piano lessons and trips to the theater when their parents couldn't afford it. As Alan began his task he was shocked to find old medicine bottles, doctors' receipts and journal entries—clues that told him too late of the illness that took her life. She had kept it a secret until the end.

> *I had all these conflicting feelings: sorrow, confusion about why she didn't let us know the seriousness of her illness, regrets that I didn't understand her better and that I didn't share more of myself with her when she was alive.*
>
> *As we packed up the boxes, I tried to get to the essential core of my feelings. I could feel the sadness. It was real, something I could live with. But there were other feelings as well—guilt and regrets that could never be resolved and were only hurting me. So I let them go. I decided to work with my sadness, to get some perspective on my real feelings about Clara.*

At a time when tensions reach a peak, many families begin to fight about "who gets what." What made Alan different is that he put his emotional energy into recasting: What was he learning about his aunt? What gifts had she left behind? What was he learning about himself, his relationship with Deborah?

*I thought a lot about Aunt Clara's life and my relationship with
her. I felt great love, great awe at her ability to carry on when she
was sick and great appreciation for who she was as a person—
her generosity to the neighbors, her ability to make friends
everywhere she went, even at the grocery store or the movies.
And I felt such respect for her. In her heyday she'd been a
successful real estate agent at a time when single women had a
hard time supporting themselves. Slowly, these feelings
surrounded the sadness, and ultimately enveloped it.*

This experience brought Alan other insights as well. Clara had
been a collector, and Alan was incredulous at some of his discoveries.
In one drawer alone, he found more than twenty silk coin purses and
scores of embroidered handkerchiefs and hand-printed scarves.

He had come to this house two days earlier with set ideas about
which objects in life were important and which weren't. By the time
he was ready to leave he had redefined his relationship to the material world. He had fully expected to take most of his aunt's belongings
home with him. In the end he took only a handful.

*An incredible part of this experience was not only what we gave
away, but the attitude and sentiments we attached to it. Piles of
old clothing, books and shoes from the fifties looked at first like
junk. But we decided that all of these things should be gifts—
not giveaways, not donations, but symbols of our esteem for
Clara.*

*Instead of calling a charity to haul it away, we went out of
our way to find people who would treasure each item. We
delivered two boxes of art books to the head of a community arts
program. The beaded necklaces she collected around the world
went to a jewelry maker we had known since we were kids. We
found a thrilled student chef who could never have afforded
Clara's expensive gourmet cookware. The old clothes and shoes
went to a theater company. And all those coin purses went to a*

preschool. By giving these things to the right people, we gave
them new meaning and new joy.

But the greatest gift was having the opportunity to know my
sister in a more intimate way. We talked about ourselves in a
way we never had before. We told family stories. We made plans
to see one another more often. We came away from the
experience feeling closer than we had in years.

About the only thing I did end up bringing home had the
least monetary value—a file of newspaper clippings Aunt Clara
had collected for years. They gave me an astonishing glimpse into
her life. From the articles, we knew she was passionate about
politics and the environment. We discovered her stance on the
death penalty and women's issues. And she had saved more
reviews of restaurants than she could ever have hoped to eat at.
This was the heart and soul of who she was—my biggest gift.

During tough times we lose too much of the experience by focusing only on the immediate tasks at hand. With so many details to
keep us occupied it is easy to skip either phase of the recasting
process—first, experiencing the feelings and second, finding new
meaning. They are both necessary and work together in tandem. The
richer your understanding of your feelings about an event, the richer
the meaning you can derive from the event.

In the end, Alan has affirmed the real love he feels for his aunt
Clara and the role she played in his life. Long after closing up the old
house and returning home, he continues to apply the lessons he
learned from her death and builds on them. He knows himself
better.

It's not having been in the dark house,
but having left it, that counts.

Theodore Roosevelt

Recasting Fear

4:00 A.M. You sit upright in bed. Your heart is pounding. You're in a cold sweat with a sense of dread and impending doom. Thoughts, feelings and images are swirling through your mind's eye. As you move from sleep to awareness you begin to feel fear. So what can you do? As an antidote to fear, recasting is a valuable coping tool.

Fear says, "I can't cope." Recasting says, "I can cope." Fear says, "I'm not going to be able to handle the bad things that are happening." Recasting says, "I can work through painful situations and emotions."

Fear is a trap. It keeps us stuck in unhappiness. It obscures analysis, keeping negative events clouded by anxiety. But working through fear can enrich us, providing new insights. By allowing our real feelings to surface, recasting helps us manage them effectively and sets us free.

What If I Lose My Job?

Sally, fifty-five, lives a wonderful life in a small coastal town between Los Angeles and San Francisco. Divorced and childless, she does administrative work at a local hospital—the only one for miles. A few years ago, an announcement was made by the hospital's new corporate owners that there would soon be a reorganization and layoffs. Like many of us who have faced job loss, Sally was overcome by outright fear.

> I was taken completely off guard, which is rare for me. I
> depended on my entire paycheck to make ends meet. I hadn't
> interviewed for a job in thirty years, and I'd lived in the
> same house for just as long. I was afraid I might have to move.
> And I'd spent most of my life with the same group of friends
> whom I didn't want to live without.

I wasn't accustomed to being fearful and it was starting to get the best of me. So on the next weekend I canceled all my plans and spent the entire time analyzing why I was so upset.

I learned something about myself that weekend—that I was becoming inflexible. I'd only lived in one place and I knew only one life. I had become too vulnerable to the fear of change.

All this wasn't going to go away on its own. So I decided to do something about it.

Sally turned fear into an opportunity to discover all kinds of new information. She began to look for ways to cope with her fears. It wasn't the layoff that scared her, it was the problems the layoff created. So, she systematically addressed each of them.

I hired a career counselor and put together a résumé—my first in thirty years. What surprised me is that I didn't look too bad on paper. I combed through the want ads and met with an employment agency. There were other jobs out there that I was qualified for. And I got all my friends at the hospital to commit to a weekly night out so I wouldn't lose them. I can't tell you how relieved I was just to know that I had all sorts of other options.

Losing her job wouldn't be fun, but now she knew she could cope with any eventuality. With this new sense of security, she felt comfortable taking some creative risks in her current job.

In fact, she felt so much happier, she impressed the new owners of the hospital with her optimism and stability. Because she wasn't worrying about playing it safe, Sally's performance on the job improved. As it turned out, she not only survived the layoff, she ended up with a better job in the same organization.

There is a powerful synergy between the first five choices in Sally's story. Her *intention* to be happy overrides her fears. She becomes highly *accountable* to herself, assuming the responsibility to take action rather than feeling like a victim of the layoff. She *identifies* what will best quell her fears. She *centralizes* by immediately doing those things that will give her a feeling of contentment. Finally, she *recasts* by understanding her emotions, learning something about herself, and then looking for new possibilities and challenges. This boosts her confidence in her own ability to handle the future, whatever it may bring.

> When written in Chinese, the word *crisis* is composed
> of two characters. One represents danger, and the
> other represents opportunity.
>
> *John F. Kennedy*

The Windmill

Sally lived through something that is known to us all: change. Change in its daily variety or change in its life-shaking form is as certain a part of our experience as is sunshine and darkness, heat and cold. In fact, we honor the inevitability of change by associating it with an inescapable phenomenon: wind. The winds of change blow continuously through our lives.

If we imagine these winds blowing around us, we can see recasting as a windmill. The wind blows—sometimes warm and gentle, sometimes cold and stormy—and as it hits us, we convert its energy into power. If our windmill is in poor condition or is completely out of operation, it will be unable to make something useful from the forceful blast. The storms of change may even hurt us. But if our windmill is in full operation, its rotors and internal machinery will meet the wind head-on, regardless of its force, and convert the gusts into useful power.

The wind is pure energy and so is the power that is generated by the windmill. The essence of the wind remains the same. But it is now a source of energy for growth, emotional well-being and nurturance. We can also store some of that energy for the future.

In much the same way, Sally has met the winds of change and, through recasting, has converted the potentially destructive blast into positive energies that serve her well. This storm has improved her present situation and given her a feeling that she can successfully recast the next blast.

Recasting Fears

The process of recasting fears can be condensed into an internal dialogue in which you give yourself permission to feel your fear fully and then put it in a context that allows you to deal with it. Follow this format as many times as you wish.

1. "I am afraid of _____."

2. "What really scares me is that I'm afraid I can't cope with _____."

3. "What would allow me to cope more effectively?" List the possibilities.

4. Which possibilities are realistic, and what can I start doing immediately?

Sometimes, the recasting dialogue does not require follow-up action. In fact, often the recasting process itself, rather than the final outcome, will alleviate your fear. The process creates scenarios, coping tools and plans, which move intense fear into the category of endurable events. Coping with those events becomes possible, so fears are reduced or erased. And there is an additional benefit: Recasting also positions you to take action.

Recasting Life-Altering Events

Imagine the many difficult events that change the texture of our lives forever: emigrating to a new country, enduring the hardship of the Great Depression, wartime military service, disabling illness, a spouse's unfaithfulness. Such events alter the way we live and, very often, the way we feel about ourselves. This is when the benefits of recasting are most apparent.

Mother's Return

At thirty-nine, Laurie was living an independent, vibrant life in the Midwest. She had a close circle of friends, was well known in the community and had a strong marriage. But that happy existence was threatened when she suddenly became the caretaker for her mother, Greta, from whom she had been estranged for twenty years.

From Laurie's earliest childhood in New England, she and her mother had been like oil and water. Laurie had always found her mother distant and cold. And, in fact, Greta had been a judgmental woman who severely restricted her daughter's social life. As a young child, Laurie was never allowed to bring other children home, nor, as a teenager, to date. When Laurie left for college in the Midwest, she never looked back.

Now, a stroke had left Greta with her intelligence and speech intact, but it had robbed her of most physical movement. She was wheelchair-bound. There was neither the money nor other family members to care for her. So Laurie was "it," and Laurie wasn't happy about it.

> At first I was devastated. I couldn't think of anything worse than having this woman dropped off at my doorstep. We were complete strangers who had barely communicated for two

*decades. I had never imagined we'd live under the same roof
again. I knew very little about caring for the physically disabled,
and I was honestly repulsed by the thought of taking care of her.*

*When she first arrived, I thought to myself, "My life is over!
What am I going to do?" But somehow I knew that the only way
to keep my life happy was to make something valuable of this
new twist of fate.*

*The first thing I had to do was to figure out exactly how I did
feel about her. It was completely clear to me that I was having
the same responses to my mother that I had as a teenager. I
thought I had gotten over her but I was kidding myself. It was
time for me to bring some emotional maturity into the situation.*

*As I began to recover from the shock of her living with me, I
saw an opportunity for us to talk to each other for the first time
in our lives. We had both changed in those intervening years. I
wanted to find out what this woman was really all about.*

Laurie and Greta started discussing how they felt about each
other. The situation was so fraught that they didn't bother to fall back
on social niceties. And as they expressed their anger openly it began
to ebb, allowing them a chance to hear one another. As they shared
stories from the past, Laurie began to see Greta as more than a one-
dimensional character but as a whole person. She was a woman who
had clearly made some mistakes, but who, in her own mind, had been
looking out for Laurie's best interests. By getting a glimpse into why
her mother had made the choices she had, Laurie's hostility gradually
turned first to understanding and finally to love and affection.

*It was a magic time, looking back on it. It was a six-year chance
to get to know my mother and myself. I experienced a kind of
acceptance of her that I had never known before. I started to
trust her wisdom and insights. She became one of my great
supporters and confidants, and I ended up loving her dearly. In
many ways, I learned to love myself more, too.*

*Mother died seven years ago. But I still talk to her in my
mind all the time. What started out as a dreadful situation
turned into one of the greatest gifts of my life.*

One of the greatest gifts for us in doing research for this book
was an opportunity to meet and know people like Laurie who have
confronted their demons and triumphed. People like Sheri, though
unhappy, were no less interesting.

In the middle of difficulty lies opportunity.

Albert Einstein

Self-Delusion

Sheri approached us after a day of corporate training in Texas. She
had heard we were writing a book on happiness, and she wanted to
be included.

*I'm an extremely happy person. My life is great. I'm always in a
good mood.*

Sheri didn't seem happy to us. Rather, she seemed distant and
uncomfortable with her coworkers. But we were always looking for
new interviewees, so we set out to qualify Sheri. We asked her, "How
did you handle the most difficult experience in your life?"

*The worst thing that ever happened to me was when I was nine.
I came home from school just when my father and two sisters
were helping my mother into the car. She was covered with
blood. They were on the way to the emergency room. Mom had
tried to kill herself with a razor blade.*

*I wanted to go with them, but Dad said, "You're the oldest.
You clean up the house." I went inside and spent hours scrubbing
the bathroom and washing the carpets. There was blood
everywhere.*

*When Mom got home from the hospital, it was never
mentioned again. And I never thought about that day for thirty
years. The best way to deal with stuff is to stay positive. That's
why I'm so happy. I didn't remember it until I was in therapy
and it sort of popped out. After the therapy, I forgot about it
again for another six years. There's no point in rehashing all this.*

*I'm not just positive about my mother. I've also stayed
positive about my divorce and my health problems. I "keep on
keeping on," no matter what.*

Sheri has repressed what must have been a horrible experience.
It's understandable that she would like to put away her sadness. Particularly as a child, she needed to continue her life without feeling the
terror of that day. But unfortunately, her denial is not happiness, it's
numbness.

Sheri is an example of what happens when people deny their
feelings about critical events. What starts off as a natural psychological response to protect ourselves from pain becomes an unresolved
issue that consciously or unconsciously colors our responses to the
world. In the end, the event has significant control over us instead of
our being in control of the event. Not feeling emotions creates the il-
lusion that everything is OK. In reality, we are maintaining a superficial mood. We can't be deeply happy because we're not experiencing
ourselves fully.

The Silver Lining

Positive thinking is a friend to all of us. Dozens of wonderful adages
advise us to see the bright side or look for the silver lining. Given the
choice, seeing what is optimistic or humorous or helpful about a
problem is far more attractive, and certainly more productive, than
dwelling on the bad part of the situation.

But there is an important limitation to the wisdom of these sayings. Some of our experiences are so hurtful, difficult or full of loss and grief that it is almost impossible to look on their bright side. In fact, there may not be a silver lining at all. The inevitable tragedies and deaths through which all of us live don't have simple solutions.

If you talk with someone who's been diagnosed with a life-threatening or degenerative disease, they will invariably tell you that somewhere along the line, a group of sincere, well-meaning people have passed along adages and positive advice. They've been told: "This is happening for a reason. You can be a model to educate people how to take better care of themselves so this won't happen to them. Don't let this get you down."

People dealing with severely painful problems, which often have a multitude of causes, need a great deal of help and support. They might recognize the warm intentions of their well-wishers, but what they really need is a clear route to get through the dark side of trauma. They want to emerge from their shock into a feeling of wholeness or wellness again.

In order to accomplish this, they need to do more than "make lemonade out of a lemon." Instead, they must first embrace the lemon for what it really is—sour and acidic, yet fragrant and colorful. It is after they experience it fully that a gateway begins to open, leading them toward healing and positive change.

Learning to Recast

This is an opportunity to begin dealing with a problem with which you're currently wrestling. But first, a few words of caution: Obviously, big problems take time to develop, and sudden traumas can wound us even more deeply. There is no "quick fix." Recasting takes time, practice and follow-through. But there is a real benefit. Recasting ultimately requires less energy than chronic suffering and grief.

Select something with which you are currently struggling. Maybe it's your biggest problem at the moment. Or maybe it's an issue that's been weighing on you for a long time.

The following is a list of questions to consider. They are examples of questions happy people ask themselves naturally as they recast. We use them during our workshops. Remember, these are *big* questions—ones that may not have immediate answers. Keep working on them.

What are the emotions I'm feeling?

Have I really allowed myself to feel all of the emotions related to this problem?

As difficult or painful as the problem may be, what things of great importance have I learned about myself (or others) because of this problem? Have I re-evaluated my life in any way?

What do my emotions and reactions teach me about myself?

Has this problem prompted me to make positive changes in my life? Or are there meaningful ways to change my life that would make me happier and more productive?

If this problem is unlikely to change, how can I best enhance other parts of my life?

Multiple Loss

As if one crisis weren't enough, sometimes there are terrible times in our lives when multiple losses pile up. You may remember the story of Adele from Chapter 1, "Intention," who experienced an unusually intense series of traumas in a very short amount of time.

In 1991 both of Adele's parents died unexpectedly. Her house burned to the ground in the Oakland firestorm, and she lost everything, including her beloved golden Lab. Her business was forced into bankruptcy by a five-fold increase in rent. Her husband had an affair and left her. Shortly afterward her best friend moved away. Adele's life had collapsed—she had nothing left.

Two choices—intention and recasting—played major roles in Adele's odyssey from emotional desolation to a greater happiness than she had ever experienced. As you may recall, when Adele hit her low point her intention to be happy supplied the energy she needed to move through an almost unthinkable amount of grief. Her intention became her commitment to live. Recasting then provided her with a way to move through loss.

At her most unhappy moments, Adele had felt that she was close to death. With so little of her life left, there seemed to be so little to lose.

> I started looking. Let's face it, I didn't have anything left to look at except myself. I remember fighting the urge to shut down emotionally. But, at the time, my emotions seemed to be all I had. I avoided pharmaceuticals. I knew if I suppressed my feelings they'd re-emerge later and I'd have to feel them all over again. Anyway, the fact that I could feel something meant that I was still alive.
>
> I forced myself to keep facing the pain. I cried a lot. I never withheld a single feeling. There was no way for me to know where I was without them. They were my signposts, my guides, my indicators. Any time I felt empty, I meditated. When I felt unsure, I called a friend to talk about it. I joined a support group for women. I wrote unmailed letters to my mom, dad and ex-husband. I poured my heart out to them. I wasn't just

feeling emotions, I was allowing them to spill over on the
written page in ways they hadn't been expressed in years, if
ever.

It was during this period that something important
happened. These tidal waves of intense emotions came up
against the reality of my losses. As they smashed together—
reality and feeling—the grief began to dissolve into something
more manageable. This was the point when I began to turn my
attention away from what was no longer—what I had lost—to
what could be. . . .

By the mere fact that I had lost all my things and my most
cherished relationships, I was stripped down to my essential self.
There was nothing blocking me from experiencing the real me.
This was the opportunity: I had the chance to build a more
authentic life for myself.

Adele began what seemed, at first, to be a near-impossible
task—to start over without external resources or support, from the
inside out. What helped her was the realization that, even with all
the loss, she still had her most cherished assets intact—her ability to
feel deeply, and her memories, skills, intellectual abilities and physical health. She also had a lifetime of rich experience to fall back on.
Slowly but surely she began to build.

Where is Adele now? She has more than survived, she has flourished. With her gourmet cooking skills she started a small catering
business that is now thriving. Insurance money from the fire provided the funds to build a serene "tree house" overlooking a verdant
canyon in the Berkeley Hills. And she has put a lot of energy into
building an intimate and warm support system of friends who will
love her and stay with her through life.

I had never really considered myself a happy person. Now I am.
In the past few years I've created a new life. I've learned to live
fully, to accept life as a whole. I'm not looking for something to

make me happy, I'm doing it for myself. I have a feeling that I can thrive in hard times. I feel content and tranquil.

What I never had before was self-knowledge. Now, I know myself. I know my limits, my emotional range, my loves. And I know I can build a life around those things. What I have now is a life that reflects the real me!

I saw sorrow turning into clarity.

Yoko Ono

Suicide—Turning a Battleship with an Oar

When my grandmother died at eighty-seven, she had lived a long, generous life. At her funeral the whole family celebrated who she was and what she meant to us. But three years ago, when my dad committed suicide at fifty-three, it was a different kind of death. . . .

By this point in the chapter you have a good understanding of recasting—particularly the drive to find meaning. But there are some events that are culturally defined as implicitly lacking in meaning, such as random shootings and early deaths from cancer or AIDS. Even if we feel the emotions surrounding these kinds of events, how do we recast something senseless?

Suicides leave behind a terrible legacy of unanswered questions. It's difficult to come to grips with this sort of void. There's no silver lining to this cloud. The next story is about Nathan's insistent search for meanings that are less apparent.

Nathan will never know why his father took his own life. His business was going along fine. Nathan and his sister had strong relationships with him. And his twenty-eight-year marriage with Nathan's mother was solid. There had been no indication that his father was in any kind of trouble.

When the call came I fell apart. I sobbed and vomited for two days. I hardly remember talking to my sister and mother. The funeral went by in a haze—I felt comatose.

Then the pain set in. A blasting headache and feeling like I had been hit in the stomach. Five days later, terrible questions started to pop into my head.

Why had Nathan's father shot himself? Was he upset, ill, in financial trouble? What had he been hiding? Was there a philosophical or moral crisis that pushed him to self-destruct? Was he depressed? If only he had left a note or talked to a friend, there might be some way to explain the tragedy. But Nathan's father had always been a discreet man, uncomfortable expressing feelings. His family was looking into an emotional black hole.

Nathan spent days and finally months searching for an answer, talking to his father's friends and business associates. But three years later, he's found no answers.

The worst part of it was the "what ifs." What if I had only called him that morning? What if I had known he was in trouble? What if I hadn't argued with him last month?

In the first months, it felt like I'd never be able to move beyond my grief. What possible purpose could I find in this whole thing? The only possibility seemed to be forgetting—let time cover the pain.

One morning I hit on the thing that saved my life. I came to the conclusion that there was no purpose to be found, and I would never find answers about Dad. What I needed were answers about myself.

Over the next few months, Nathan took his search farther afield. He made promises to himself. He pondered the nature of father-son relationships and began to treasure even more deeply his relationship with his four-year-old son. He vowed to be as open as he could with

his child, to break family patterns by establishing as intimate a connection as he could with his son. And he pushed himself to be more
honest than he had been before. He grappled with the ethics of suicide, his father's lack of concern for others, and grasped how precious his own life was to other people. He responded to his new
feelings of responsibility for his mother and sister by making himself
more emotionally available than he had been in the past.

Things were not the same for Nathan's mother and sister. They
had been hit equally hard by the suicide. Devastated, they at least allowed themselves to feel their pain. But they never got past the facts.
They spent months, and ultimately years, pondering the "whys" of the
death.

> *I worry they'll never get past the crying stage. They are still in*
> *shock. Their lives have come to a depressing stop.*
>   *It's not that I don't still feel the effects of all this. I do. I don't*
> *think I'll ever lose my sadness. It's a part of me now. But I've*
> *grown from Dad's death. It's helped me answer some questions*
> *about life for myself. What I've gained is a feeling that my life is*
> *precious. Every minute counts. I don't take anything for granted,*
> *and I don't get caught up in all the b.s. anymore.*
>   *This has been the hardest thing I've done in my life. More*
> *difficult than turning a battleship with an oar. But I did it.*

> I think the years I have spent in prison have been the
> most formative and important in my life because of the
> discipline, the sensations, but chiefly the opportunity to
> think clearly, to try to understand things.
>
> *Jawaharlal Nehru*

Recasting stands alone among all the choices of happy people
because it works specifically with events that leave us profoundly unhappy. Whereas the other choices generate new, increased happiness,

recasting restores happiness when it's been taken away. As such, it is an essential skill. Without it, we can make all the other eight choices but still be unarmed to deal with crises.

So now what? Recasting teaches us that we can not only survive but also thrive during a difficult time. We begin coming out of a dark tunnel, but into what?

We're ready to take a plunge into the multitude of wonderful things life has to offer. We're poised to open up options.

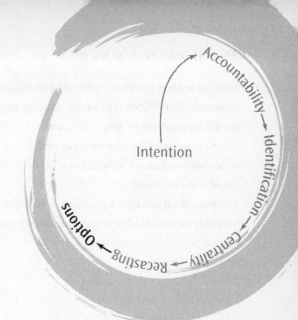

Chapter 6

Intention → Accountability → Identification → Centrality → Recasting → Options →

Options

I'm free when I allow my life to unfold. As soon as I restrict myself to known outcomes, I've got a noose around my neck.

Adele Goldstone, caterer

Keep on sowing your seed, for you never know which will grow—perhaps it all will.

Ecclesiastes 11:6

Happy people thrive in an ever-changing world by opening up their lives to a daily bounty of possibilities. Rather than sticking to the straight and narrow, they are inspired by a multiplicity of paths regardless of how unusual those paths may be.

Pushing beyond the obvious, they don't settle for doing things in the most accepted way but strive to uncover any and all approaches. For them, the exciting part of life is the journey, not the destination. Confident in this attitude, they set off each morning on a voyage of personal exploration, unburdened by predetermined goals and expectations.

Travels with Robin

For happy people, every experience offers a new chance for adventure. A business trip, the open house at their child's school or even a much-dreaded family reunion are seen as offering possibilities and potentialities that can't be anticipated in advance.

Robin, a forty-one-year-old piano teacher, loves her rich and varied life, which integrates all the things that interest her most: performing in children's shows, working with people she likes, giving classes. Robin relishes travel and prides herself on having taken "blue highway" trips through all fifty states.

> For me, life is really about the side trips. Sometimes that unplanned bathroom stop along the route introduces me to a town that turns out to be the highlight of the trip.
>
> When I travel I stay incredibly loose. Never had an itinerary, never will, so I can take advantage of wonderful and bizarre things that present themselves. One great thing leads to another. When I come into a small town I go into the first shop I see and ask, "What's the best thing in town?" It could be the out-of-this-world meat loaf at Hilda's Diner or the boat rides some guy gives at a nearby lake or the twelve-foot-tall dinosaur that

someone's built in his front yard. I've met such great people and
experienced wonderful things.

This is the stuff that brings joy to my life. The way I travel is
really a model for the way I live. It's all about celebrating the
unknowns. I don't like to create expectations for my day. In fact,
my one and only daily expectation is that all kinds of new and
wonderful things will happen. It's my way to stay open to all the
possibilities. This way, rather than being disappointed when
certain things don't happen, I'm delighted at whatever does
happen. . . .

Most of the people I know aren't even aware of where they
could have gone. They go from one place to the next without
paying attention to all the fun and experiences they could have
had getting there. So many people miss the twelve-foot
dinosaurs.

Not every happy person we met was quite as spontaneous as
Robin. Some prefer a more detailed planning process and structured
schedule. But there is one thing they all have in common with her:
They are never rigid about their plans. They don't assume that things
have to go a certain way, and they are willing to approach each day
with flexibility. To them, rigidity causes unhappiness.

You can plan events, but if they go according
to plan they are not events.

John Berger

Convergent Versus Divergent Thinking

When we approach any decision—traveling or otherwise—we use
two different kinds of thinking. One is convergent thinking, the quick
elimination of possibilities until only one exists. Our social training
teaches us that this is the most effective way to think. Making a "snap

judgment" is a common kind of convergent thinking; so is honing our route down to only one way of getting from Point A to Point Z.

Happy people approach life differently. They use divergent thinking, the consideration of many prospects without a sole outcome in mind. This is discovering possibilities and developing scenarios. They told us, in effect, "The conclusion will take care of itself."

Let's use two fishing strategies as examples.

Since we are all traveling in fundamentally uncharted seas, we have no way of knowing what experiences life will bring us in the future. So how do we fish in life's waters?

If we were to use *convergent* thinking, we would first identify the kind of fish we want to catch. Then we'd drop a single line into the water, at the proper depth, and wait to hook the "big one." This approach has some distinct disadvantages. We may have to wait a long time to get a fish with the right profile. And much to our frustration we may never succeed. Another downside is that while we're focused on our one goal, we fail to experience the marine circus playing above and below our hook.

But if we were to use *divergent* thinking, we'd toss out a net without a specific fish in mind. Who knows what we'll haul in? With so much activity in the water, we're bound to land something interesting. As we happily sort through our catch, we can choose which fish to keep and which to throw back.

Chance is always powerful. Let your hook always be cast;
in the pool where you least expect it, there will be fish.

Ovid

Tossing the Net

Jason, newly married, is a twenty-five-year-old computer programmer. Sometimes on Sunday mornings, he gets up early and spends a couple of hours at the open-air flea market near his home. He doesn't necessarily go to buy things. Instead, he goes for the adventure.

I feel like an urban archeologist. I particularly love the old paintings and photos. I like to study them, figure out who the people are, get a glimpse into their lives. The old family portraits are the best.

Every time I spend a couple of hours at the flea market, it leads to something else. I've taken watercolor classes. I've become interested in Eastern European culture and turn-of-the-century American culture. . . .

The flea market fires Jason's imagination. One day, after fishing through every booth, he was attracted to a faded watercolor being displayed among old posters and paintings. Captivated by *Paris—1948,* as the painting was called, Jason bought it from the obliging owner for two dollars. It was a sunlit street scene with the Cathedral of Sacre Coeur in the background. Jason had never been to Europe, so the painting represented the Paris he had always imagined and wanted to see.

Like all of the objects Jason enjoyed at the flea market, this painting opened his mind to another place and time and sparked his curiosity about Paris, French culture and architecture.

Most of us would stop at the fantasy, leaving the thought behind. However, this is where divergent thinking made the difference. All the way home in his car, Jason found himself thinking about the possibility of actually going to Paris.

Something about this painting really grabbed me. Maybe it was its similarity to all the old MGM back-lot scenery that had framed Leslie Caron and Gene Kelly. Who knows? But, I thought, why don't I make a few calls tomorrow about the cost of a trip for my wife and myself? The worst thing that could happen is that we wouldn't be able to go and, you know, I was already not going. What did I have to lose?

Jason cast his net. Rather than falling back on a notion of what was realistic, he went to his travel agent and checked out all the options. Could they possibly travel to Paris at Christmas time? In fact, he found that since this was off-season, he could get great bargains on air fare, hotel rooms and rental cars. Jason also investigated cheap flights to other cities, deciding on a whim to add Barcelona—and all for the price of a two-week trip in the United States.

> *I couldn't believe I was going to Europe. The minute we hit Paris, we set out for Montmartre, to find the site of my painting. When we came upon it, we were in heaven.*
>
> *The boulangerie was still there. It hadn't changed in over fifty years—right down to its awnings and shutters. When we ate lunch in the restaurant in my painting, I told the owner about my odyssey to Paris. He suggested certain museums in the city, where I would find more paintings of the same street. The museums, in turn, led to some amazing explorations and adventures in neighborhoods I hadn't imagined and of artists I hadn't known before.*

Jason's exploration continued after Paris. In Barcelona, at the outdoor market, "Els Encants," he spotted another tiny watercolor, this time of a seaside town. It was the kind of picturesque village he'd noticed in travel books and dreamt of seeing in person. A concierge at his hotel identified it as a painting of the exquisite medieval town of Tossa del Mar. You can guess where Jason and his wife went the next day.

There is nothing magical or coincidental about this story. It is the kind of story that we often heard from happy people—a simple willingness to stay open and a refusal to allow obstacles, either real or imagined, to get in the way. This is what leads to adventure.

Any time we let our negative assumptions guide us, we shoot ourselves in the foot. "We probably can't afford it." "He'll never say yes." "I think they have a policy against that." If we give in to all these doubts, what happens? We end up staying home rather than going to Paris!

———

Live! Yes! Life is a banquet and most suckers
are starving to death.

Patrick Dennis, Auntie Mame

———

A Divergent Career Path

Engineering is a profession known for its structured career path. Yet, in southern California we met seventy-year-old Phyllis, who created a fulfilling forty-five-year career in engineering by using divergent thinking. At each step in her professional life, Phyllis remained inquisitive about new directions that might enrich her growth. She was always looking.

Now semi-retired and living with her husband in Santa Barbara, her interests are still extensive. As one of the early women in engineering she is proud of her groundbreaking achievements.

> *When I was starting out there was a myth among engineers that there was only one way to be successful, that there were certain "benchmarks" that told you if you were on course. Once you got your engineering degree, you moved up the ladder by becoming a design engineer and next a research engineer. Then you became a project leader, followed by engineering manager. The ultimate benchmark was vice president of engineering.*

Early in her career, Phyllis was burdened by the benchmarks. She felt compelled to achieve a specific professional level at a certain age and earn a specific salary at a certain time. If she didn't hit a benchmark according to schedule, she thought of herself as a failure, particularly if her male counterparts hit the benchmark first. Not only did she try to stay on their path, she tried to act like them, talk like them and be one of them.

I was miserable. So I dumped the master plan. We were all competing for the same thing, and it wasn't something I wanted in the first place. I had already broken the rules by becoming a female engineer. Why was I following them now? So I became an explorer! I wasn't going to be happy until I aligned my career with who I really was.

Who was Phyllis? She loved engineering but she also loved a lot of other things. How could she combine her interests into a career? She did it by staying open.

At the time I was a project leader and found the job description limiting. So I figured it was time to cast about for a new direction. I answered an ad to write articles for an engineering magazine because I'd always loved to write.

She didn't get the writing job because she was overqualified. Instead she was offered a far better position as research director for the journal. Three years later, she began to write a column under her own byline.

I was delighted. Writing about engineering put two of my interests into alignment. The job lasted five years. And during that time I tried my hand at a lot of things. I tried editing. I was a liaison with publishing houses. I was a marketing rep for the magazine. Some of these I liked, some I didn't. And I have no regrets. The point is, I kept moving. Any one of these choices was far less important than the fact that I just kept choosing.

I have a philosophy: Any choice can be reversed, but not choosing at all is irreversible.

Here's the bottom line. Things don't get figured out in your head, they get figured out in the process of life itself. The only way to find joy is to let your life unfold. When I do I find myself in a place that's different from anything I could have ever imagined.

Because she had made so many contacts, Phyllis was becoming well-known. The president of a large engineering firm was so impressed with her variety of talents that he offered her a vice presidency in charge of client relations. Phyllis took the job with the proviso that she could keep writing her column. This was another big jump in her career. Within five years, Phyllis became the president of the company—to this day an unusual accomplishment.

> *At this point in my life the fewer specific goals I have, the happier I get. When I used to carve out goals, it actually ended up making me miserable. As soon as I stopped benchmarking, I got a lot happier. For me, benchmarking takes all the fun out of life.*

Phyllis has taken on the role of explorer. But what happens when we follow a rigid path? Can we succeed? Can we be happy?

———

The choice may have been mistaken, the choosing was not.

Stephen Sondheim, from his song "Move On"

———

A Convergent Career Path

Like Phyllis, Darrell is also an engineer. For twenty-five years he has worked successfully for a municipal government in Florida. In spite of his success, he describes himself as "not particularly happy." When he was in his early twenties, Darrell mapped out a detailed professional plan that he followed without compromise. Now, at fifty, he's mapped out the rest of his career as well. Darrell is sure this plan will eventually make him happy.

> *Security has always been my goal so I've got my entire life planned out. I knew that staying in one profession would get me the benefits I need for retirement. I won't make it to the next level for five more years. Then when I'm fifty-five, I'll be ready to move to another company in a senior management position. By*

that time, I'll be too old to go much higher. So at sixty, I plan to get a job teaching engineering and public policy. I'll have enough money to retire at sixty-five and do what I really want to do.

What does Darrell really want to do? He doesn't know. If he follows his plan to retirement, he's got fifteen long years in a job that gives him security but isn't what he wants to do. Darrell is sure that this plan is "the only way it can be." And he easily offers ten reasons why no other approach will work.

Why is he so unhappy? Because he's locked into his own plan, unwilling to consider any other possibilities. And what's his favorite gripe?

It seems like nothing ever works out for me. Some people are just lucky and others aren't. I'm so tired of being disappointed by life.

Darrell often feels disappointed because he accepts what life throws at him as "just the way it is."

Q: "What do you see yourself doing five years from now?"
A: "I have no idea. I've never had a career plan and never will. I just always make sure that I'm doing something I love at the moment, and I find out where it takes me. I float downriver, then I wake up and say, 'Oh, here I am. I've had a swell float.'"

Diane Sawyer, interviewed in US *magazine, Sept., 1997*

The Risk of Flexibility

Darrell brings up a reasonable issue: security. Let's consider the opposite of security: risk.

Is it riskier to follow one path or to explore a number of scenarios? In his search for security, Darrell presumes to know precisely what is going to happen in the future. But the future rarely happens exactly as we expect. On Darrell's narrow path, every change means disappointment. In fact, Darrell told us that he is always anxious about unforeseen events that might foil his plans.

Happy people would say the security-minded Darrell is actually putting himself in great jeopardy. Even though he might not think so, he's taking a terrible risk by planning a single scenario. He hasn't hedged his bets. In reality, he may be far less secure than the people he considers to be big risk-takers, those who don't live by one plan.

Darrell's inflexibility leads to a more stressful and less satisfying life. Imagine an actor finding out he's been given a leading role. He runs to the bookstore and buys the script. The actor goes home, locks himself in his room and methodically memorizes his lines until he's sure he has mastered the perfect interpretation. He says to himself, "That's it. It's flawless. I'm done."

Then rehearsals begin. He's so certain he has completed the task that he doesn't listen to the other actors; he doesn't key off them; he's not open to discovering new interpretations; he's not mindful that the story is taking a new turn. As adept as the actor is technically, he is an unhappy participant in this production. He fails to understand that he's part of a much larger set of circumstances that are constantly in flux and have a dramatic impact on the way his character unfolds. Even though he knows everything there is to know about his character, nothing seems to be going right for him. He doesn't feel connected because he's not keeping up with the growth and development going on around him.

You are lost the instant you know what the result will be.

Juan Gris

Lost Tickets, Gained Opportunities

William is a happy guy with a wife, two teenage children and two poodles, living near Union Square in the heart of New York City. Big-city life can wear you down. Unexpected problems seem to pop up every time you turn a corner. But William has a survival technique.

Every time I hit a disappointment, I say, "OK, what's the opportunity here? Can I change my perception so that I see the problem in a new light? What choices do I have?" The funny thing is I usually end up with something better than what I thought I wanted in the first place.

William told us about what had happened the day before. He had gone to the box office of one of the hottest Broadway shows in town. Knowing that it was sold out for the next few months, he decided to try his luck. Persistence had usually paid off in the past. Sure enough, his timing had been perfect. Two tickets in the orchestra section had just been returned for that evening's performance. He rushed to the phone to notify Heidi, his thirteen-year-old daughter and theater companion, who was thrilled at the chance to see the show.

But in the midst of all this excitement the tickets disappeared. William thought he must have dropped them running across the street. The box office cashier remembered which seats had been sold to William, but because it was a cash sale, there were no guarantees he could see the show. Someone else could find the tickets and show up to take his place. The theater promised to do the best they could to help.

I was so mad at myself. I thought about how disastrous the evening might turn out. So I fell back on the old standby: "How can I find an opportunity here?"

It took me all of fifteen seconds to see the opportunity clearly. Heidi and I could make an adventure out of the evening. There was now an excitement about how the evening would play itself out. Would there be someone in our seats, and who would they be? How honest would they be? In fact, what would their story

be? How did they get the tickets? Where would we end up?
Maybe the theater would find us even better seats.

There were so many alternative plots to this adventure. The
potential for great stories seemed far more interesting than just
seeing the show.

The postscript to this story: William found his tickets a few
hours later buried in the inside pocket of his jacket. However, during
those intervening hours, looking beyond the immediate problem and
seeing new prospects had allowed him to go about his day without
feelings of stress and disappointment.

Creativity, Limitations and Boredom

Traditionally, American culture has taught us to work hard and stay
on the straight path to reach our goals. Parents, teachers, clergymen
and bosses tell us never to lose focus, keep our noses to the grind-
stone, keep our heads down but our chins up. Frankly, we'd have to
be contortionists to do all this at the same time.

If there were a single voice speaking for our society, it would tell
us that productivity, not happiness, is the number-one agenda item.
And as society's largest representative, the corporate world trains us
to be productive by setting "specific, measurable, achievable and realistic" goals. They would say that the hallmarks of a successful person are to be hardworking, financially secure and goal oriented. This
may represent success, but it is not happiness.

If we look back over our lives at our most thrilling accomplish-
ments, they were likely things we never dreamed were realistic or
measurable. But we gave them a shot anyway. Happiness requires this
kind of unfettered creativity. If we only do things we already know to
be achievable, we will rob ourselves of some of our greatest moments.

When you step away from the confines of "realistic," you become an artist painting your own masterpiece, an explorer charting new territories. You are creating new ways of looking at situations; you innovate at work and at home. It's impossible to be bored.

Living is a form of not being sure, not knowing what's next or how. The moment you know how, you begin to die a little. The artist never entirely knows. We guess. We may be wrong, but we take leap after leap in the dark.

Agnes de Mille

I Don't Have Options

Many of us feel we don't have a lot of options. Our responsibilities confine us. Our jobs trap us. We think we're too poor or too old or too tired to create life changes. And we have limited time and resources.

To happy people, limitations are challenges. And how do they rise to the challenges? Creativity. They are much like sculptors who envision beautiful shapes and forms inside rough blocks of granite. Give them what appears to be nothing and they revel in the search to make it something. Each new day presents the potential for relationships, education, personal growth, professional development and just plain fun.

Do you feel that you have limitations? You're right. The truth is whether you're an independently wealthy person living on an estate or a federal prisoner doing a life sentence without parole, your life is replete with limitations. You also have a multitude of options.

In our public workshops we use an exercise to prove, on the most basic level, that we always have options even when we believe otherwise. Here's how it works:

Partners face each other in chairs and have ten seconds to study one another. Then we instruct them to position their chairs back-to-back. Their assignment is to change five things about themselves that others can see.

Typically, a low groan fills the room. "I can't think of five things!" Yet, with a little thought, most find a few solutions. They often switch their watch to the other wrist or maybe unbutton a button. And if they're really daring, they take off a shoe. Then their partners try to guess what's different about them. It is interesting to note that at this point in the exercise most people feel awkward. Many are already anxiously placing their watch back on the "correct arm."

Guessing what's different is not the real object of this activity. The point is made with the next step. We ask them to position their chairs back-to-back again and to change ten more things about themselves.

This time the groans are decidedly louder. They shout, "Impossible!" So we say, "You won't be successful unless you get really creative. Take risks. Think outside the box. Get wild and crazy!" Most people seem to need this kind of permission to break through their own barriers in order to open up a whole new set of possibilities. Once they feel free to do so, they're not only able to change ten more things, some can change twenty or thirty or more.

By the time the exercise is over, we're looking out over a sea of innovation. Participants are grinning from ear to ear as gym socks hang from the sides of sunglasses, belts are wrapped around heads, shoe laces are tied around fingers and shirts are worn backward. In spite of their initial resistance, the demure, well-dressed group we started with have been abundantly able to transform themselves.

This exercise is a metaphor for life. There are so many more possibilities than we allow ourselves. They can be endless. We just need to let go of any preconceived notions about what they are and then start searching.

What are the risks? Just like in the exercise, you might not want to risk looking silly. You might feel uncomfortable. Others might

think you're unattractive because, after all, you've changed your carefully designed public image. And you might have to see yourself differently. If you're like people in the workshops, you'll forget about
what others think and you'll start enjoying yourself.

Finding New Options

You can learn to explore more options whenever a challenging
situation arises. The steps to follow:

1. Recall a recent situation you found disappointing. This should
be something that didn't turn out the way you wanted it to. Envision every detail, explore every feeling you experienced during
that situation. Make the picture in your mind as clear as possible.

2. What was your level of awareness as you walked into the situation? Were you on autopilot? Envision other options in the situation that might have made it more bearable or even turned it
into a great opportunity. List them without being judgmental.
Sometimes some of the most unusual ideas turn out to be the
best ones. See how many you can come up with.

3. Could these options have helped you create a happier situation? What got in the way?

The key to exploring your options is awareness. If you are aware
that you can create options and possibilities at any time, you will
be looking for them. You can do this when life is pleasant or
when you hit a roadblock. In either case, new options can make
life happier.

Helen Keller, Abe Lincoln,
Albert Einstein and J.R.

For the most part, the heroes we love best are those who triumph over limitations—the physically handicapped Helen Keller; the impoverished young Abe Lincoln; and Albert Einstein, who pushed far beyond the intellectual and theoretical limitations of turn-of-the-century physics. And then there's J.R.

Even though he is unlikely to become a cultural icon, at fourteen J.R. was dealing with all the limitations of his suburban teenage life. They may have been more commonplace than those of Keller, Lincoln or Einstein, but nevertheless, to realize his dreams J.R. had to examine his life to overcome limitations of age, geography, money and peer pressure.

His mother, Mary, describes J.R. as very different from her first child.

> J.R. was such a serious, focused and not particularly happy
> infant. But by the time he entered kindergarten, we had ceased
> being normal parents who guide their children through each
> decision. He was so independent that we became merely advisory
> to him. The best way to describe J.R. was curious. And the more
> he explored his curious nature, the happier he got.

J.R. was a middle-class kid growing up in New Jersey. By the time he became a teenager he felt restricted by the conformity all around him. Now at twenty, he looks back:

> At my high school there was only one way to look and act. You
> were supposed to be good-looking, play sports and wear certain
> brands of clothes. I knew there was a whole world out there, and
> I was only being exposed to one tiny part of it. I wanted new
> ways of doing things and perceiving things. I figured out the best
> way to unlimit myself was to spend time out of the country in a
> whole new culture.

As soon as he proposed a plan to study abroad to his parents and school officials, J.R. hit a wall of serious objections and limitations. The programs were expensive, and his parents could not afford the outlay. And they felt that at fourteen he was too young to be away from home. Anyway, most of the study abroad programs were for juniors and seniors only. His friends began to ridicule him for wanting to leave the crowd: "How could you go to some foreign country and not hang with us?"

But he forged ahead, eventually becoming the only sophomore ever to be accepted in a program that would allow him to live and study in an Argentine village—a far cry from New Jersey. How did J.R. deal with the roadblocks? He opened up options on every front. To raise money he gave tae kwon do lessons out of his garage. He found a local organization to sponsor him. And he learned Spanish from audiotapes.

Once he arrived in Argentina, J.R. continued to push the limits. His hunger to experience the wonders of the world led him to blaze new trails that left the program directors in awe of his resourcefulness, particularly when it came to his weekends off.

An excursion to the Beagle Channel at the southernmost tip of South America was a prime example. Instead of taking the tourist boats to tour the channel, J.R. asked around until he located a man with a small boat who would take him places most people never get to see. The guide turned out to be a freelance photographer for the *National Geographic* who provided J.R. the chance to see the region through the eyes of an artist. With camera in hand J.R. spent the next five hours taking brilliant photographs of the channel. What he learned that day about form, color, light and composition spurred him on to other experiences in the visual arts—another example of one scenario giving birth to many new opportunities.

Another time, when all the foreign exchange students were scheduled to fly to a conference in Buenos Aires, J.R. cashed in his plane ticket and ventured out solo on a three-hundred-mile trip on the local bus system. He spent two days out of touch with his anxious adult supervisors, socializing with the "locals" and getting a firsthand view of the countryside.

His mother sums it up best:

J.R. is never one to do it the easy way. I'd hear stories from Argentina and say, "My God, I hope he comes back alive." And he did—more alive than when he went.

Now a college junior with a double major in psychology and biology, J.R. was recently chosen to be a researcher in a prestigious behavioral neuroscience study. He had first developed an interest in psychology from his host father in Argentina, who was a professor of psychology at the National University. J.R. plans to return to Argentina next year to do his graduate work in alternative medicine.

J.R. is a rare human being. Curiosity informs his life as it leads him to explore the world's intricate offerings. Not surprisingly, such curiosity leads him directly to an intense appreciation for life.

Whatever is flexible and loving will tend to grow;
whatever is rigid and blocked will wither and die.

Lao Tzu

Chapter 7

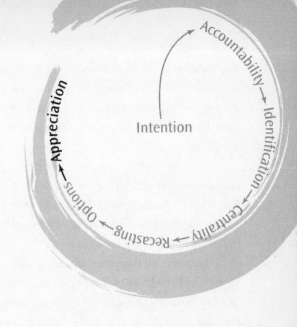

Appreciation

Intention · Accountability → Identification → Centrality → Recasting → Options → Appreciation

There isn't a day that goes by that I don't think . . .
I can't believe I'm here. This is so wonderful!

Leslie Darin, historian

The roots of all goodness lie in the soil of
appreciation for goodness.

The Dalai Lama

Appreciation is many things and assumes many forms. Appreciation is transformation. It is awareness. It's how we acknowledge others. It's the way we open our emotional floodgates and let our happiness flow into the world. And appreciation is our way of living fully in the moment.

With appreciation, we move mountains. We can take what is ordinary and turn it into something special. We can elevate a friendship into a great relationship; disarm a business adversary, make a crisis more bearable; balance sadness with beauty. How? By seeing what there is to appreciate in any situation.

Happy people have unusually acute vision, an ability to see life clearly in all its diversity. They've an awareness of contrast—good and bad, beautiful and ugly, soft and loud, fast and slow. They notice the beauty of a flower and see the ugliness of poverty as a counterpoint. They have a consciousness of form—hard, soft, angular, flat—the daily symphony that plays all around us, the sweet sounds of its music contrasted by the harshness of the jackhammer. And they get perspective from values—right and wrong, weak and strong, righteousness and evil. They embrace loved ones for their greatest strengths and for their most troubling faults.

This depth of field gives happy people a special view of what there is to appreciate around them. Their awareness of what's happening is mixed with an intention to be fully immersed in life. They take time to notice, to really see—breathing deeply, experiencing, savoring what is right there in front of them to enjoy.

Appreciation like this is existence in the moment. Nothing is taken for granted. Life is a gift, and happy people look for what can be appreciated now. When they find it, worries from the past and anxieties about the future fade against their Technicolor experience of the present.

The logic behind all this is clear. It's a physical fact that, no matter what happened an hour ago, a week ago or what might happen in a year, happiness can *only* be felt now, in this moment. It can't be experienced any other way. We can anticipate the future and we can remember the past, but it is only in the present moment that we can feel.

Happiness comes when we attach what is happening in the present to our immediate feeling. It's not getting overwhelmed, for example, by nostalgia for the past or anxiety about the future. This would dampen our experience of what is happening in the moment.

The notion that happiness comes from living in the moment has been validated for centuries by our ethical, religious and philosophical heritage.

This is the day which the Lord has made.
Let us rejoice and be glad in it.

Psalms

The secret of health for both the mind and body
is not to mourn for the past, not to worry about the
future, nor to anticipate troubles, but to live the present
moment wisely and earnestly.

Buddha

Do not worry about tomorrow's trouble, for you
do not know what the day may bring. Tomorrow may come
and you will be no more, and so you will have worried
about a world that is not yours.

Babylonian Talmud, Tractate Yevamot

Let's face it, in spite of thousands of years of philosophy, living in the moment is much more easily said than done. Our busy lives are enveloped in a swirl of events just passed, with new ones impending. The ephemeral "now"—that millisecond between then and soon—is hard to grasp. So how do we develop an awareness of the moment and the ability to see what there is to appreciate?

Consider William. He may have had a tenuous hold on Broadway theater tickets (Chapter 6), but his grasp on the present is strong.

The Good Scenes and the Bad Ones

For William, appreciation is a way to make all parts of his life into a rich personal experience, even taking him far enough to see the comedy within a tragedy and the pathos in a comedy. Movies are his metaphor.

> *I like to think of my life as a movie with thousands of vignettes—tiny scenes that fit together to create a dramatic and intriguing story. And I'm thrilled that I get to be the star.*
>
> *I look at every episode in my life as just the next scene—it might be good or it might be bad, but it's the next experience I get to have. I like to appreciate each scene for what it is. Whether it's comedy, drama or tragedy, I value it because it's a part of my unique story.*

Not only is William the star of his movie, he's also the audience. To fully enjoy his life he becomes involved in each scene as it happens, experiencing it exactly as it is, not how he wishes it might be. Like the avid audience for *Hamlet,* William doesn't resist tragedy but, rather, embraces it as another of life's experiences. When life turns comedic, William is laughing like the rest of the audience at what is happening at that moment.

The idea that life unfolds like a script has served William well. Just before our interview, William and his coworkers had made a major sales pitch. In spite of weeks of preparation, their client was unimpressed. This was a blow to the entire team.

> *I sat in that meeting knowing that the presentation wasn't being met with any enthusiasm. But rather than seeing all those late*

night and early morning meetings as a waste or worrying about how the boss was going to react, I focused on the "now."

As I looked around the table I could see my colleagues working hard to turn the situation around. I had such gratitude for their professionalism and tenacity. I could also see the quality of the presentation materials we had brought along and felt pride in the teamwork that had gone into producing them. I even appreciated the humor in watching the clients respond so impassively to the frantic energy we were putting out.

As William anticipated, the story didn't have a particularly happy ending. Yes, the team lost the deal and the boss was furious. But by not labeling this a "terrible event," William had been able to appreciate it as a whole. Would he purposely repeat the situation? No. Did appreciation allow him to see more than a disaster? Yes. It was a situation with fantastic highs and lows—a roller-coaster ride full of variety, intensity and richness.

When we fight against the totality of our lives, we risk missing life altogether. William's brand of appreciation takes into consideration that no experience is entirely bad or entirely good. No event is without something that can be appreciated. No feelings ever go to waste. And here's the good news: Unlike just about everything else in life, there's no down side to appreciation. It never works against us.

———

Best to take the moment present,
as a present for the moment.

Stephen Sondheim, from his song "Any Moment"

———

The Traffic Jam

During a workshop in California, Josh was struggling with the entire notion of appreciation—particularly with the idea that there's always something to appreciate in the moment. He challenged us with: "OK then, how do you appreciate a traffic jam?" We responded with a challenge of our own and a homework assignment: Consider your appreciation possibilities the next time you are stuck in traffic. Then get back to us.

A chemist, Josh reported back in the form of a time-based scientific analysis.

> *I spent years cursing my miserable commute each morning. It turns out to have been a total waste of time. I found an answer to your question. Now, instead of the twenty-minute drive from hell, I spend twenty minutes thinking about and appreciating all the marvel in my life: I'm in love with the woman of my dreams. I've been improving my relationships with my family. I'm taking much better care of my body—I'm doing yoga twice a week. I live so close to beautiful hiking trails.*
>
> *I made some calculations. If I add up all my commute time over the next fifteen years I can spend more than twenty-six hundred hours being angry at the world or appreciating it. I've made my choice.*

If Josh sees himself only as a frustrated man caught in a traffic jam, there's not much to appreciate. But if the same man caught in traffic is also a person with loving relationships, a fine professional life and a love of nature, there's a lot to be grateful for.

Josh has enlarged his own awareness of self in the moment. As he's driving he is appreciating the marvelous life of the expansive, engaged and intelligent man in his car—himself.

To be alive, to be able to see, to walk . . . it's all a miracle.
I have adapted the technique of living life from
miracle to miracle.

Artur Rubinstein

Blues in the Night

During the day he is upbeat, proactive and feels quite content. In his waking hours he is a happy person.

But as darkness falls so do Alan's spirits. He often awakens in the middle of the night feeling depressed and sad. This is part of a diagnosed family-wide pattern of "low-level physiological depression." He describes this sensation as a "dejected humming" in his brain.

There are times when the mild depression amplifies into an intense feeling of confusion and disorientation. As he becomes fully awake, these feelings coalesce into a sense of dread about every unresolved issue in his life. This is when he is visited by the ghosts of the past and future. Will he have enough money to send his kids to college? Will his cholesterol count be lower at his next exam? Could he have spent more time with his aging parents?

Until recently, sleeplessness was taking a toll on Alan. His doctor prescribed sleeping pills, but they left him feeling dopey.

> One night, I got angry with myself for not being able to control the whirling rolodex of issues in my brain. "Hey, you don't feel this way during the day. Why do you have to feel like this at night?"
>
> I think out of pure frustration, I forced myself into daytime-mode and began to feel grateful about all the good stuff—my kids, what I was going to enjoy in the morning, even imagining the smell and feel of a hot cup of coffee. Somehow, I quieted that compulsive ranting in my brain.
>
> Now I've refined the technique. It can be difficult, but I think of all the things I can appreciate at that moment. The warmth of the bed . . . the coolness of the pillow beneath my head . . . the sweet night breeze.

Alan starts to feel a distinct change in his body—as though "everything is readjusting." His head clears, the depression diminishes, his body relaxes, and he falls back to sleep.

> *But when my appreciation technique fails, it is a flashing red light alerting me to take action in the morning. . . . The irony is, though, that just sorting out the real problems from the other stuff usually makes me relax enough to fall asleep.*

There is no question about it—behaving in certain ways makes the body feel better. It is a cycle. For Alan that cycle begins with his conscious choice to appreciate. By doing so, he is creating a change in his mood that he experiences as a feeling, a body sensation. As he relaxes, the biochemical changes that have taken place allow him to fall asleep. The next day, because he feels rested, his mood is elevated. This leads him back to a choice—appreciation—thus completing the cycle.

It is Alan's consciousness of the choice to appreciate that sets him apart from most of us. Nonetheless, he is experiencing a sudden positive change in his biochemistry that we would all recognize. Think of how happy we feel in body, mind and spirit when we receive some unexpected appreciation. We feel physically invigorated and emotionally elevated. As we've said before, emotions and physiology are simply two sides of the same coin, so highly integrated that they should really be seen as one.

Yesterday is ashes; tomorrow wood.
Only today does the fire burn brightly.

Old Eskimo saying

Being in the Moment

Write down three times in your life when you have felt the most alive. These experiences will be different for each of us. Maybe it's when you were skiing down a slope. Maybe it's when you embraced the tempo of a bustling city. Maybe it's when you were quiet and by yourself in nature or when you made a deep connection with another person.

Why is it that you felt so alive? Was there a "rush" from the experience? Were you completely focused on that one event, without regard for the problems that cropped up yesterday or the presentation that you have to make at work tomorrow? If so, you were probably "in the moment."

Appreciating Others

If you want to turn an everyday experience into a memorable event, try this the next time you're having an ordinary midweek lunch with friends. During the meal, look up slowly, push back from the table and say, "I want you to know how much I appreciate you as friends. You make work (or life) so much more fun. It's so nice to be with people I can trust and depend on. Having your support means a lot to me and I want to thank you." Watch your friends' faces. Chances are they'll burst into smiles! You will have created a special moment.

Maddie is well known for making special moments. You were first introduced to her in Chapter 1 as the neglected child growing up in Hollywood. She has come of age. To understand her depth of appreciation, you must know who Maddie is now. As an adult she is generous of spirit, intelligent and capable of deep appreciation. She is a lovely, compassionate human being who has become a well-known broadcaster in the Northeast. The community loves her for her high-profile, on-air fund-raising campaigns. She practices a kind of "down home" appreciation. Because Maddie's use of appreciation is so panoramic, we are using her as the representative voice of happy people in the myriad ways they appreciate others.

Visiting Maddie in her station's newsroom is like walking into a hurricane.

> *We work on very few "good news" stories. Most of the time we've got tragedy, scandal, natural disasters. How do I keep myself happy? I use appreciation as a survival technique.*
>
> *I did most of the station's coverage of the Oklahoma City bombing. Several times each day I paused to acknowledge all the wonderful small things that were happening around me—the community courage, the bravery of the rescue workers, the skills of the medical team. By appreciating the good, I was able to stay balanced in the middle of the horror.*

To Maddie, appreciation is not passive. There are three components in her process. First and most important, she actively looks for the opportunity to appreciate. Then she allows the feeling to fill her—she really feels it. Third, she goes the extra distance and expresses the feeling out loud.

> *It feels so great to express it. I send the flowers right at the moment I feel the appreciation, or I stop what I'm doing right then, pick up the phone and say, "I was just thinking about you so I called to tell you." I believe that when you appreciate the good in others, the good grows stronger.*
>
> *I tell people how they've touched me and the impact they've had on me. Sometimes I say it; sometimes I write it. I keep a pile of white note cards with me wherever I go. Throughout the day I'll grab one and scribble a quick thank-you—to waitresses, the*

*charity volunteers, the mail room staff—to anyone who goes that
extra step and does or says something that really makes a
difference to me.*

Maddie confirms what we've learned from our consulting: Appreciation can be one of the most powerful forces in a productive workplace. Yet with all their emphasis on productivity, we haven't encountered a single corporation that makes a practice of appreciation.

We're committed to it. When we run team training programs in large corporations, we often facilitate thirty-second exchanges of appreciation between coworkers. Believe it or not, this exercise often elicits tears from these adults. Even hard-boiled executives break down. Why? Because they have spent years in an environment rife with criticism, harsh evaluations and negative feedback. We all want to feel valued for our contributions. If thirty seconds of appreciation has this extreme effect, imagine the power appreciation would have on a daily basis. So why doesn't it happen? Because most people don't think it's their job to appreciate others. Or they're simply too embarrassed to express it. Or it hasn't been encouraged by the corporate culture.

In reality, giving one another positive recognition is one of the most important things we can do. Just hearing a few seconds of appreciation forges stronger relationships. And often, what is being appreciated are the little things that typically get overlooked such as attention to detail, a sense of humor or creativity on a project. By contrast, the lack of appreciation is one of the major reasons people choose to leave their jobs.

And what about appreciation for our loved ones, the people who mean most in our lives? Maddie's practice of appreciation affirms the pattern we saw throughout our interviews.

*When I appreciate the people closest to me I'm wishing them
well. I am grateful for what they mean to me and for who they*

are. And it's not just the good parts of them. I put myself in their
shoes by appreciating their struggles and their fears. I acknowl-
edge them for trying to be better people and for doing the best they
can, for their gentleness and for their aggressiveness. Even in times
of conflict I try to appreciate them for their anger and frustration,
because even though it may be unpleasant, it means they care.

I want to be comfortable with the differences between us
instead of being threatened by them. Appreciating people for
themselves is the best way I know to create love.

One of the most important outcomes of all this is empathy. In
the worst of times, when the relationship is in trouble or a problem
has become overwhelming, appreciation creates a gentle space. It pre-
vents us from losing sight of everything we value and love about the
relationship and keeps the current problem in perspective. It nurtures an opening, a point of caring and love that might initiate a step
toward intimacy and growth. When we feel appreciated, we can let
down our guard and find mutual points of agreement and acceptance. Even though this may be the time we least feel like appreciating someone, it is probably the best, most important time to choose
to do so. It is a time we can choose to feel the texture of the relationship instead of glossing over the surface. It is also something we might
try to do more regularly. Consider it a gift to a loved one.

Actually, as a culture, we do have designated days of appreciation. Thanksgiving is a day of appreciation. We officially appreciate
our veterans, our country's birthday, our mothers and our fathers, not
to mention our secretaries and bosses. Our most sacred religious holidays are about appreciation—the birth of Christ, the lasting power
of the oil in the lamp, the passing from slavery to freedom.

Happy people don't wait for official holidays. Many of them
create their own rituals. Maddie has a yearly tradition.

I throw myself a birthday party and have each friend bring a toy
which I donate to a social service agency. It gives me a chance to

*be grateful for the people in my life and the joys they give me.
But most important, I get a chance to appreciate myself on that
day—and what better day to do it?*

Underlying this urge to appreciate is a fundamental sense of
self-worth and significance that is critical to our feelings of happiness.

*Growing up in the kind of household I did, I had such low self-
esteem. To this day, I have an old, childhood voice in my head
that kicks up every now and then when something good happens
to me. "Do you really deserve this? You're not worthy of this.
You're not a good enough person." The guilt kicks in and
threatens to sabotage me. My solution is appreciation.
Something good happens, boom, I move to gratitude. I don't
judge it, I just appreciate it. It works every time.*

You say grace before meals. All right. But I say grace before
the concert and the opera, and grace before the play and
pantomime, and grace before I open a book, and grace before
sketching, painting, swimming, fencing, boxing, walking,
playing, dancing and grace before I dip the pen in the ink.

G. K. Chesterton

Disarming an Adversary

*Until last week, getting one dollar of funding from this woman
meant putting up with her sour expressions and mean-spirited
questions. She's like a gargoyle. I couldn't stand being in the
same room with her. Then something happened.*

Jolene is the director of a nonprofit agency that is funded by a
corporate foundation. Jolene saw the foundation head, Mrs. Heath, as
a combative woman who seemed to enjoy making life difficult for
every grant recipient. In the past, just anticipating a meeting with

her made Jolene tense and angry. But things had suddenly changed for the better in the week we had a follow-up conversation with Jolene, a participant in one of our workshops.

At the workshop, Jolene had rated herself at the low end of the appreciation scale. It was something she didn't pay much attention to in her personal life and hadn't even considered in her business life. But aware of the possibility of using appreciation as a tool for change, Jolene walked into the yearly meeting with Mrs. Heath, along with the directors of four other nonprofit organizations.

> *As I expected, there was absolutely no agreement amongst us on the issues, and Mrs. Heath was in rare form. But I had promised myself to actively appreciate everyone's viewpoint.*
>
> *I was so used to blocking Mrs. Heath out, that I had to change my entire mindset. As I started to find things to appreciate, I began to calm down. I took the attitude that everyone had something important to share. Even though I didn't agree with much of what Mrs. Heath said, she had a perspective that could be helpful to me. I really felt under control and in a positive mood for the first time in this situation.*

When Jolene got home she decided to go one step further. She wrote each person a letter. In the letter she thanked them for their time and for sharing their individual perspectives, and she told them what she had learned.

For Jolene, the process of writing the letters was transformative. She actually had been grateful for their participation and stayed open to a variety of viewpoints instead of tuning them out. But an unexpected "gift" arrived several days later.

> *I got a call from Mrs. Heath thanking me for the letter. We had our best talk ever. The conversation was collaborative for the first time because we both lowered our guard and talked honestly.*

There was another spin-off. Jolene got thank-you calls from every other person at the meeting, which strengthened all of their professional relationships. But the biggest payoff was much more personal—Jolene's own exhilaration at the way she had handled the situation.

Let me embrace thee, sour adversity,
for wise men say it is the wisest course.

William Shakespeare, Henry VI

Learning Appreciation

Choosing appreciation can become as fundamental to your life as eating and sleeping. It is simple in practice but requires heightened personal awareness. The three steps of this exercise suggest a way to find what you truly appreciate and how to act on your feelings.

1. With a timer set on five minutes, speed write a list of everything you appreciate. Dig down and empty your brain onto the paper. Avoid self-censoring. Don't worry about being silly. Your list will probably include simple items as well as bigger ones—relationships, life experiences and physical pleasures.

When the timer sounds, stop and allow yourself to feel whatever emotions you may be having. Pay attention to those feelings. What do they tell you?

2. Review your list and make a note next to each item. Decide whom you need to appreciate. You may want to thank a higher

source for the kind of life you lead or the people who have most influenced your life. And don't forget to appreciate yourself for being who you are.

3. Right now, what is there to appreciate in the moment? Try to deepen your awareness of the present.

Each part of this exercise should provide you with a deeper consciousness—a meta-awareness—of what you appreciate and how you need to express that appreciation. Try doing this exercise every couple of weeks. See what happens.

Loving Myself

Happy people seem to know other happy people. For us, finding one usually meant uncovering a succession of others, often stretching across the continent. This is the way we met Judith—great cook, hostess *par excellence* and storyteller.

One of Judith's earliest memories of her much-loved father is walking with him hand-in-hand down the lazy streets of Louisville. Inevitably, they'd get home late because en route he'd stop to appreciate a robin's nest, the odd pattern of a tree trunk or the summer clouds racing by.

> *He always took time to notice how wonderful life was. But now, with an adult's perspective, I know that he must have been living a nightmare. My mother was in and out of mental hospitals for as long as I can remember, and he had to be the sole emotional and financial support for all four of us kids. Appreciating the beauty in life had to be one of the ways he survived.*

Forty years later, Judith stood with her father on a hotel observation deck overlooking the Las Vegas desert.

He broke out with a smile and said, "Judith, isn't life absolutely wonderful." That moment is the picture I will always carry in my heart. No matter how terrible things were, he never lost his ability to love everything that was happening to him. He was my greatest teacher.

Appreciation goes way beyond noticing the pretty things and the happy things. It may sound strange, but I truly appreciate that I'm capable of having feelings of sadness about my mother who's been institutionalized with schizophrenia since I was ten. The more I've learned to appreciate these feelings, the more I've been able to appreciate and love myself for my emotional depth and maturity as a woman, for my strength in living a successful life and for my ability to continue loving a woman who couldn't be a mother to me.

Appreciating ourselves is a way to honor ourselves. It's an acknowledgment that we consider ourselves to be important, worthwhile people. Judith's appreciation of her own depth of feeling is an affirmation of her capabilities, her uniqueness as a person. It's her way to heal the wounds left by a lifetime of rejection from an unstable parent.

Why do so few of us actively appreciate ourselves? Because somewhere along the way we were taught that self-congratulation is egotistical. Someone told us we weren't being "humble" when we commended ourselves. In reality, appreciating ourselves is anything but egotistical. It's a quiet echo reminding us of who we are.

Whether we use appreciation as a means of staying in the moment, a method of transforming a difficulty or a way to be more loving, it becomes a gift—something we give to ourselves and to others.

Earth's crammed with heaven.

Elizabeth Barrett Browning

Chapter 8

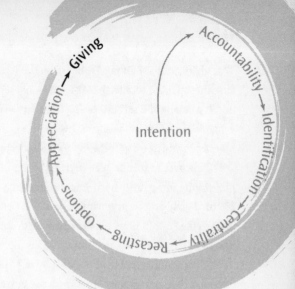

Giving → Accountability → Identification → Centrality → Recasting → Options → Appreciation → Giving

Intention

Even though I don't expect it, when I give from my heart it always comes back to me in wonderful ways. That's the way of life.

Reuben del Rio, hotel bellman

God loveth a cheerful giver.

II Corinthians 9:7

Giving

True giving, radiant giving, comes from the same inner place as deep happiness. It's a desire to share our personal sense of worth and values. It's having the self-esteem to feel that what we have to offer is valuable—our advice, wisdom, expertise, skills, physical labor. The manner in which we give these gifts is a reflection of who we are.

Nowhere is this better portrayed than in the twelfth-century philosophy of Spanish-born Jewish philosopher Maimonides, who pictured giving on eight spiritual levels. His *Code* ("Laws Concerning Gifts to the Poor") offers a comprehensive description of the ways we give to others and how our giving is received.

To Maimonides, whose philosophy reflected thousands of years of Jewish thought, giving comes from the heart and soul and is at its best when disconnected from the earthly concerns of greed, guilt and duty. Like all the nine choices of happy people, the motivation for real giving finds its source in the internal self, not in the expectations of others.

What Maimonides described in the twelfth century is alive and well in modern life. The kind of giving he describes plays a big part in the lives of happy people. Even though it is unlikely that any of the people we talked to have studied Maimonides, virtually all of them have made his highest levels an integral part of their lives.

Maimonides's highest level is supplying a source of livelihood to someone in need, thus allowing him to become free of dependence on others. If we translate this into modern terms, it means giving so that people can live better, more independently and more effectively. To that end, happy people told us about being involved in mentoring programs and job programs for the poor and needy. Some talked about volunteering at hospices to help people live through the ends of their lives with a degree of dignity and independence. Others are active members of family and community, giving advice and counsel generously from their hearts.

The second-highest level in Maimonides's schema is anonymous giving, in which neither the giver nor the receiver knows the other. He points out that this eliminates both the hurtful possibilities of shame and embarrassment on the part of the receiver and self-aggrandizement by the giver. This is the notion of giving without reward.

In fact, happy people don't expect a return. They give because it is a decree of their heart, letting their internal sense of contentment and joy overflow into the world. They want no other payoff. The more they give, the happier they feel, and the happier they feel, the more they give.

But there is a striking paradox. Beyond the personal emotional returns, giving *does* bring a myriad of tangible rewards—in the form of strong community, people networks and deeper relationships. To happy people, though, this is a secondary consideration—the frosting on the cake—and certainly not what drives them. The substance of what motivates them is the basis for the stories in this chapter.

Our society is constructed to encourage us to give. There are many rewards for our generosity, from the tax deductions we receive for charitable donations to the recognition and prizes we receive for our community work. But there's a problem: This system sets us up to expect recognition and rely on external acknowledgments. And then when we aren't acknowledged, we feel disappointed, maybe even used. Sometimes, in spite of these feelings, we continue to give. Often, it's because we think we should give.

This obligatory giving violates the fundamental impetus of every happy person with whom we spoke, and it is Maimonides's eighth and least spiritual level of giving, which he called "giving morosely."

The reward of charity depends entirely upon
the extent of the kindness in it.

Babylonian Talmud, tractate Sukkah

Small Gifts

There is an enchanted form of giving that we see in small, personal acts of kindness. This is generosity of spirit on a level so personal, so modest, that it goes unnoticed in our busy world. But it is happening all around us, quietly making the fabric of our lives a little better.

We found these captivating acts of giving throughout the entire economic realm of happy people. Whether rich or poor, happy people find ways to give that are often unrelated to personal wealth or material items.

Reuben, twenty-seven, doesn't have very much money. Surviving on the salary of a hotel bellman, he helps support his Puerto Rican family of nine living in the Bronx.

> *I want to make the world a better place in any way I can. I see unhappy people all day long—their faces are turned down with frowns. These may be selfish people—even bad people—but I don't care who they are. It is not for me to judge any of them. I look into their eyes and give them big smiles. I talk with them. Everywhere I go—on the street, riding the bus—I share my joy with them. I can see I've given them the gift of a little kindness. Even if it is just for a minute, it is something they can enjoy. Maybe I have helped change their lives a little.*

Reuben told us about an unusual relationship he has with an isolated eighty-five-year-old man. George has no other friends or family and lives on social security benefits in the building next door to Reuben's hotel. Their unlikely friendship began six years ago on the sidewalk in front of the building. For the next year they would meet on the street and have far-ranging discussions. As time passed, George grew less mobile and ultimately became a shut-in. So Reuben started to visit after his working hours.

> *George was once an architect and he knows so much about everything. I like to see him every day. In a funny way he keeps*

*me going. When I bring him groceries he tries to offer me money
but I don't take it. That's not what it's all about. I feel like I'm
the lucky one because I've learned so much from him. I'm there
for him, he's there for me. I love him.*

These are the small gifts we give one another. They are, in fact,
the kind of love and kindness that binds us together in the most personal ways. They are the mortar of our world.

If I can stop one heart from breaking,
I shall not live in vain;
If I can ease one life the aching,
Or cool one pain,
Or help one fainting robin
Unto his nest again,
I shall not live in vain.

Emily Dickinson

Musical Chairs

One of the exercises we often use in our happiness workshops is called
"The Musical Chairs." By rotating through two lines of facing chairs,
everyone in the room has the opportunity to talk individually with
everyone else. The instructions for the exercise are simple: "Give each
person in this room a gift."

We frequently get resistance up front. People tell us, "But I didn't
bring anything to give." "I don't know these people well enough."
"What could I possibly give?" We tell them to be creative. "You have
something to give to each person." The exercise begins with some re-
luctance and skepticism.

As musical chairs comes to an end, the room erupts with laughter and enthusiasm. Toward the end of a long day, this exercise leaves
people feeling energized, upbeat and excited. What did this group

have to give? All sorts of things! A simple act of appreciating their partner of the moment. An offer to help with some professional advice. A compliment. An invitation to lunch. A bit of support for a previously expressed emotional issue.

The feedback we get from individual participants is enthusiasm and amazement. "It was so easy. I feel great about what I heard, but even better was realizing how much I could find to share with others."

Exploring Giving

We will let the twelfth-century expert Maimonides be our guide as we explore our own experience with giving. For the purpose of this exploration we will look at the kind of giving he considered to be the height of blessedness.

Before you begin, it is important to know that as the levels of giving descend they become increasingly entangled in the foibles of human ego—greed, envy, insincere obligation and peer pressure—making them increasingly less significant to you as sources of happiness. But if you give at the highest level, you will be replicating the experience of happy people.

Make notes as you give yourself some time to explore.

The Highest Level of Giving: Giving so that another can support himself/herself without dependence on others.

> What can you do to help others enhance their ability to support themselves?
>
> Are there ways you could mentor, give someone the "tools of her trade" or teach life skills?
>
> Could you help people live more independently?

If you are currently involved in this kind of giving, how does it feel?

If this is something you might consider doing, can you imagine how it would feel?

There are no easy answers in the world of giving. We are pressured to give all day long. But we can increase our happiness by giving openly, honestly and from the heart.

Rolling up Your Sleeves

Stone, forty-seven, an international management consultant, gave us a great deal of his time during three separate interviews, a flow of faxes with articles about happiness and a handful of referrals to other happy people.

There are so many opportunities all day long to give, if I just make myself aware of them. Very often it's not money or belongings that people really need. It's things that can't be seen— advice, resources, compliments, feedback. These are things that are so easy for me to give, and they provide me with a lasting sense of value to the world.

Stone was a representative member in the choir of happy people. We heard a continuous refrain from them: Giving is not limited to writing a check at Christmas time, it is about physically getting involved, rolling up the sleeves and plunging in.

I love to feel the thrill of physically doing something with others to help the community. It's something I do all the time.

Last week I called a volunteer group who put me in touch with a young woman who heads an organization for crack-

addicted mothers. Just getting the chance to work with her and to experience her energy was in itself astounding.

I went out and bought two cribs with sheets and blankets and set them up at her clinic. Every step of the way I felt connected to other people—the store manager gave me a discount; other volunteers at the organization rallied to assemble the beds. A fantastic feeling of warmth grew between us. The giving was contagious.

My rewards are limited only by my ability to recognize them. There is no greater joy for me than watching people that I've affected flourish. I see the baby in the crib with my pink blanket. I see the mother's smile, the glistening eyes. I get a hug of thanks. A trust develops between us, and the intimacy, if only for that moment, that comes from "being there" for someone warms my heart and I'm high as a kite. Giving is a game that everyone wins.

It is one of the most beautiful compensations
of this life that no man can sincerely try to help
another without helping himself.

Ralph Waldo Emerson

Giving gifts to others is wonderful. But sometimes we give in a way that diminishes us. And why do we do this? The simple response is guilt. We believe that somehow we haven't done enough for someone, so we'll expunge our guilt by giving until it hurts. We have "too much" and our guilt drives us to give it away. This behavior has many names—self-denial, self-abnegation, martyrdom—but it all falls under one category: sacrifice. This was an issue Annie had to face.

Leftovers

We met Annie through a high school administrator who dubbed her the "happiest faculty member in the district." And, in fact, once we did some research we found that her generosity and sense of content- ment are well known throughout her school district. An English teacher, Annie, age sixty, considers herself the happiest person she knows. But she wasn't always this way.

> *Happiness is something I've learned in adulthood. In my age group, women were raised to self-sacrifice, to put themselves and their desires aside in favor of others. Now I find it hard to believe, but when I was a girl, sacrifice was what we referred to as "giving." And I was taught that I should make sure to get credit for my "generosity."*
>
> *There is a story that has stuck with me. When I was first married I used to host lavish dinner parties for family and friends. At the end of the evening I would always wrap up the leftovers for my guests to take home. The truth was I wanted to keep the food for my own family.*
>
> *Nevertheless, I gave it away to get brownie points. I wanted people to consider me a generous person. I had been taught to say, "Oh, it's nothing," when, in fact, that wasn't true.*
>
> *It's clear to me all these years later that I was playing a very unpleasant game. I ended most of these evenings feeling used—I was "giving," but I resented it.*
>
> *These days I keep the leftovers. And when I'm complimented on my cooking I simply say, "Thank you, I love doing it." And I genuinely mean it. I don't need to get credit anymore because I give myself the credit. I'm my own judge.*

Today Annie's giving is extensive but looks very different from those little foil-wrapped packages of leftovers. She is considered an educational guru in her community. Having taught English literature and composition for many years, she shares her rich professional skills with younger teachers throughout the state of California whom she invites to her classroom.

> *I love to share what I love. I consider this the most powerful kind of giving. I say to them, "What are you teaching and what do you need? My files are open; here's what I've got. Take anything you need." And then we head for the copy machine. Why would I not give kids and teachers the benefit of my experience? It's certainly not taking anything away from me.*
>
> *I encourage new teachers to leave my office with boxes of material that I've developed over the last twenty-five years. It makes me feel wonderful that I can contribute so substantially to someone's growth.*

As we've said before, overcoming our childhood conditioning can be an important step in becoming happy. Giving is a complex behavior, made even more complex because we receive so many cultural messages about how, where, when and why to give. But giving in its purest form—as when a father shares something of himself with his son—is powerful in its directness and authenticity, and it has the potential of changing the entire course of a lifetime.

Kindness in words creates confidence. Kindness in thinking creates profoundness. Kindness in giving creates love.

Lao Tzu

A Gift from My Father

On his deathbed, Hiroshi Tanaka's father made a demand of his four young sons. *"Promise to find knowledge. It will open up your world and give you a route to freedom and happiness."* Many years later, Hiroshi would look back and realize his father had given him a gift that would last a lifetime.

At the time of her husband's death, Hiroshi's impoverished mother was forced to split up her children between family in Japan and American social service agencies. The year was 1931, the depths of the Great Depression, and a time of deepening resentment against Japanese Americans. As the youngest child, eight-year-old Hiroshi was sent to a foster home in Arkansas; his three older brothers were sent back to Japan to live with relatives at their ancestral home in Hiroshima.

Though displaced and alone for the rest of his childhood, Hiroshi never forgot the promise he'd made to his father, as he nurtured "an insatiable appetite to learn."

In my earliest memories, I felt a growing sense of security as I got my education. Even though my new world was alien, nothing scared me. I felt close to my father. And that security gave me a sense of power and confidence. I felt I could have the whole world in my hands.

Hiroshi graduated from high school in 1941—a period of intense anti-Japanese feeling. Without any way to pay for a college education, he volunteered for the U.S. Army and was sent to school by the military at the University of Oklahoma—one of the few institutions that would enroll Japanese Americans. In spite of the acute racial prejudice he experienced at school and in the military, he graduated after the war with a business degree and began a stint in a U.S. government agency. It was during this time that he reunited with his siblings—all of whom had survived the war.

In 1954, Hiroshi decided to use his business education and open a carpet-cleaning business. To break into the market he published an ad that read: *I'll clean all the carpets in your house for $1.* It was a marketing technique that paid off. The calls came pouring in. In a few short years he built an extremely successful business, eventually employing more than thirty part-time workers from the nearby college.

I reached great success at an early age. This was not an accident, but a direct result of my business education. My father's gift to me—a promise demanded more than twenty years previously—had paid off. It was time for me to pass along his gift to others.

Hiroshi became a mentor and father figure to many of his employees. Education was his passion and the gift he gave to them. Regardless of the workload and his own economic pressures, he allowed employees time off to study for exams, tutored some, and gave others interest-free loans for tuition.

He glows with pride as he talks about their later achievements. Among them are politicians, doctors, artists, businessmen. One even became an ambassador. Dozens of them have remained in close contact through the years, and to this day he counts them among his closest friends.

I tried to mentor every employee who needed help. I spent time with each one of them, coaching them to stay in school, teaching them all about business, about customers and sharing skills I'd learned from my own experience. I had so much love to share. I wanted to give them the knowledge and tools to become whatever they wanted to be.

Now in his seventy-fourth year, Hiroshi tells his favorite story, which involves Donald, who came to work for him as a directionless and struggling young man.

I liked Donald very much and felt he had a lot of potential. When he stopped working for me I remained close to him and helped him get into military school. Several years later he came to me and said, "Hiroshi, I just want you to know I'm going to be your competitor. I've decided to open my own carpet-cleaning business right here in town."

Rather than discouraging the competition, Hiroshi told Donald he'd like to help. And with his extraordinary urge to teach he showed

Donald every trick of the trade. With Hiroshi's blessing, Donald not only became Hiroshi's biggest competitor, his company became one of the largest and most successful carpet-cleaning businesses in the United States.

This is my proudest achievement—when my gifts helped other people find fulfillment. I have passed along my father's gift—the gift of education—to another person. This is my greatest joy.

Life begets life. Energy creates energy.
It is by spending oneself that one becomes rich.

Sarah Bernhardt

The Commerce of Giving

Hiroshi's story illustrates what we call the "commerce of giving." Try to imagine the constant flow, the give and take, that happens in a "giving marketplace." It is a marketplace into which generous people offer their "goods"—whatever they want to share with others. These goods may include skills, emotional support, material items, money or time. Into the marketplace come people who have needs that match the available goods. They feel invited to take what they want and are then moved to give something back. The giving and receiving become part of one cycle. Everyone participates in this community-wide phenomenon, and the marketplace grows.

Hiroshi is a wonderful example of a marketplace participant. He was given the "gift" of invaluable advice from his father. He then shared the gift with many others, who, in turn, gave the gift of happiness to Hiroshi. It is certain that many people who received Hiroshi's gifts passed them along to others in an ever-growing marketplace.

But what happens when you break the cycle?

Kathryn's Story—Part Three

(continued from Chapter 2)

My life had turned the corner. I hadn't been this happy in years. The bulimia was gone. I had a wonderful group of dance instructors working for me. My rental space was becoming a popular spot for nighttime dance parties. I was getting a lot of support around town from other studios. And, best of all, I was dancing.

Then I moved into my own ballroom—10,000 square feet of converted warehouse space! It had to be the most thrilling moment of my life. And for the first few years after the move my business was blessed. My only problems were the usual small business issues—accounting procedures and payroll systems.

At that point I was training a group of my own extremely talented dance instructors, pouring energy into them. Many of them had already built individual followings among the ballroom's students.

Then I started to hear the whispers. Some of them were quietly planning to go out on their own—to open new studios.

I felt betrayed. My mood plummeted. How could they do this to me? I had given them everything and they were turning on me. And anyway, this was a cutthroat business—I thought these renegades were threatening everything I'd worked so hard to create.

I retaliated in panic. I stopped their training immediately and used every business tactic I knew to block their new businesses. I started to divide and conquer and took each of them aside and tried to talk them out of going out on their own. I did everything I could to divert them away from their aspirations. My feeling of happiness was crumbling and I knew why.

I was swerving back to blame. I was telling myself that the instructors were making me unhappy. Obviously, it wasn't them. I was doing it to myself.

I had lost my bearings. I'd abruptly stopped giving anything to anybody. My life was focused on negative behaviors. It was now all about money, manipulation and control. I felt miserable trying to stop all these people from realizing their dreams just because I felt economically threatened. So many people supported me when I first started out. None of my teachers tried to stop me from opening my own business or prevented me from realizing a dream. This wasn't what I wanted to do to someone else.

It didn't take me long to see how much I was hurting people who were dear to me. But, more than anything, I was feeling terrible about myself. I learned something—that doing business is not about blocking competition. It's about making my own business the best it can be.

I had the presence of mind to do an about-face. I apologized. I started to teach them again and to support their plans. Some finally did go off on their own. Some stayed. But my relationships with all of them have remained strong.

Coming out of that experience I've done a complete about-face. I've learned something about myself. Even though dancing is still a thrill to me, I've found that my greatest happiness comes from developing dance instructors. I love helping them become fabulous teachers. When I bring an instructor to the point that she can go out on her own it's my ultimate accomplishment.

(To be continued in Chapter 10)

Giving to others becomes a gift that happy people actually give to themselves. From a business standpoint, Kathryn and Hiroshi both believe that by encouraging and coaching others, goodwill comes back to them many times over. Hiroshi has had tremendous economic success against the odds of racial prejudice, family financial standing and geographical disruption. And despite the fact that eight other dance ballrooms have opened in her city during the past few years, Kathryn's business is still growing.

But far more important than their business successes, Hiroshi's and Kathryn's stories illustrate how external priorities like economics, competition, monetary success and recognition pale by comparison to the choice of happiness.

The greatest good you can do for another is not just to share
your riches, but to reveal to him his own.

Benjamin Disraeli

Information Is Power. Or Is It?

Hiroshi's and Kathryn's stories reminded us of our work with corporate teams. More often than not, we work with people who hold on to a belief that is pervasive in industry: Withholding information creates power.

In our experience this is no more than a corporate wives' tale. The most successful and happiest business people we know *share* information, they do not withhold it. By sharing with colleagues they create a powerful network of people who trust and support them in the workplace. This kind of sharing creates a giving marketplace inside the corporate walls. Those companies with an information-sharing culture have high trust levels—a major contributor to greater employee satisfaction and productivity.

Cheerful But Not Happy

There were times during our research when we got referrals to happy people that didn't quite pan out. Rich was one of them.

He told us about his eighteen-month recovery from a rare nerve disease that had left him temporarily paralyzed. Rich had been referred to us by an architect who was among hundreds of people in Kansas City who volunteered to attend him during his slow but successful recovery.

Rich's illness aroused great community sympathy, and offers of help flooded into the hospital. For over a year he was fed, clothed, bathed, read to, turned in bed and wheeled through the hospital by well-wishers who voluntarily took four-hour shifts around the clock. Through it all he was known for his determined cheerfulness and positive attitude, which made him a promising candidate for an interview.

As our referral source had suggested, Rich was upbeat and engaging. He had received so much. What impact did this outpouring of love and support have on him? Was he engaged in the commerce of giving?

> I appreciated all the help I got. But I've moved on. At this point in my life I'd like to forget the whole episode ever happened. I personally have never thought much about giving. I guess we'd have a hard time saying no to any of the people who helped me at the hospital. But otherwise I can't think of any other way I really give except maybe that my wife and I occasionally have people over to the house.

Considering Rich's attitude toward the dozens of people who had helped him through his own illness, we were skeptical that he experienced happiness as a deep, enduring feeling.

> I've always been a jovial sort of guy—even as a kid. My whole family likes to joke around. But am I really happy? I don't know. I think life's tough and you do the best you can. If happiness means giving away the store, then no, I'd rather not be happy. . . .

Rich clearly has a biological set-point that keeps him cheerful during difficult times. But the kind of profound, long-term happiness we have found in others has eluded him.

The Ballad of Billy Lee

Billy Lee's story seems borrowed from a country-music lament. At sixty-five, Billy owned a limousine service in the Deep South and took great pride in his automobile. Late one night he stopped at a neighborhood gas station to wash his hubcaps. As he stood up with a bucket of water in his hand, he saw a young man pointing a gun at him across the car's hood. Reflexively, Billy threw the soapy water in the man's face. As he began to run, an accomplice positioned behind the vehicle shot Billy twice in the back.

It was a terrible decision on my part. All they could steal was my watch, wedding ring and seven dollars cash.

Billy was rushed to the hospital. His wife and three grown daughters were told he would die. Miraculously, Billy regained consciousness after eight days in a coma. For the next four months he made a slow but successful physical recovery.

During that time, Billy found himself living in an unfamiliar world of anger and hurt. Nothing seemed right anymore. He struggled to reconcile what had happened to him.

These feelings lasted until the trial of the young man who shot him. Billy Lee's twenty-one-year-old assailant was given a thirty-year sentence. When the verdict was announced a resounding cheer echoed through the courtroom. But Billy wasn't after revenge. Looking across the courtroom at the young man's grief-stricken parents, he instinctively moved into the marketplace of giving. Flooded by a feeling of compassion, he walked across the room to embrace them.

The three of us just held each other for I don't know how long. Then we sat down and talked about the shooting—what it had done to me and them. We had all shared a great sadness. From that point on they were a part of my life. I told them I'd "be there" for them and I was. We got together many times after that.

By spending time with them, that terrible question, "Why did this happen to me?" faded away. What we did was help each other. This is how I healed.

We fly frequently to Billy's city, so we get to see him often. We've spent hours with him talking about happiness. Every ride in his limo is a delightful experience. When he stops to pay a toll, Billy hands a candy bar to the toll-taker. He does the same wherever he goes—giving packets of gum, a smile or a kind word to whomever he meets. These are small things, but, as his companions, we can feel the effects of his giving. He creates a warm glow in everyone he encounters. Losing Billy would have been a sad event for our world.

If you want others to be happy, practice compassion. If you want to be happy, practice compassion.

The Dalai Lama

Although we heard hundreds of stories about how happy people give, one characteristic held true in every case—truthfulness. Truthfulness is the standard by which all giving is validated. For giving to come from the heart it must be an honest expression of ourselves.

Chapter 9

Intention

Truthfulness → Accountability → Identification → Centrality → Recasting → Options → Appreciation → Giving → Truthfulness

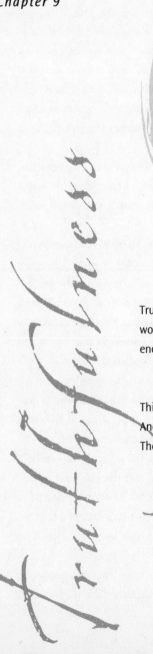

Truthfulness

Truth guides the way I relate to the rest of the world. I know what's true for me. And that's enough.

Annie McAvoy, English teacher

This above all: to thine own self be true,
And it must follow, as the night the day,
Thou canst not then be false to any man.

William Shakespeare,
Hamlet

We bring the circle of nine choices to completion with "Truthful-ness." The choice to be truthful is a rich and deeply personal state-ment that happy people make *about* themselves, *to* themselves. It is a kind of truth that speaks to the ability to confront our personal mythologies, to look at our behavior honestly, and to do what is right for ourselves, regardless of the social pressure to do otherwise. This fundamental honesty to ourselves also becomes the wellspring of truthfulness with others.

Ironically, the most cherished American fable about honesty is, itself, a fabrication. Regardless of its authenticity, the story of George Washington and the cherry tree simplifies truth into a simple edict: "Don't tell lies!"

In fact, we do tend to tell the truth to the world at large. With-out social truth-telling our entire world would fall apart. Almost all of us conduct our lives without cheating other people at the grocery store or gas station. We don't steal flowers or fruit from outdoor stands. We fulfill our contracts and obligations. This type of honesty is part of a social compact to which we adhere so that our world won't be fractured by theft, graft and corruption.

Unfortunately, in our most important relationships we often assume that we need to be strategic, discreet and withholding to pro-tect ourselves. From what are we protecting ourselves? If the truth were told, we fear rejection, retaliation and embarrassment.

But not telling the truth to ourselves and others is the source of many of our greatest problems. Without truth there can be no real in-timacy in our most important relationships. At work we don't feel genuine. We lose connection to our children. But, most important, we lose contact with our true selves. Can we, in fact, know ourselves if we don't tell the truth to ourselves?

It's not always easy to tell the truth to ourselves, but when we do we've achieved a feeling of personal integrity. The world seems "right," and we feel happy.

If one can actually revert to the truth, then a great deal
of one's suffering can be erased—because a great deal of
one's suffering is based on sheer lies.

R. D. Laing

The Internal Contract

When we make a commitment to tell ourselves the truth, we have
forged an internal contract. Having the idea that truth is a personal
contract is where extremely happy people seem to have a special corner on the word "truthfulness." They are adamant about understanding their own "truths" in any situation. They test their reactions
to people and problems. They are searching for what is real in their
responses to life. In short, they strive for authenticity and accurate
personal evaluation—to exist in a state of integrity with themselves.

Mercedes came to the United States as a spirited teenager after
living the first years of her life in the outskirts of Mexico City. She
spent five years in the Southwest learning to speak English, and another three learning computer basics. Her hard work paid off. Now,
thirty years later, she is the respected head administrative assistant in
a computer company.

> *Truth is the contract I make with myself. It's not always easy, but
> honoring it makes me happy. It has evolved over time—it has
> become my belief system and essential to who I am, my
> foundation. It's what I can come back to, it guides me. . . .*
>
> *When I experience something that goes against this truth—
> with who I want to be—lights and buzzers go off in my brain
> and heart and stomach. That's my signal to re-evaluate. Truth is
> a motivator for me. It keeps me on a straight line, on track. It
> helps me when I'm floundering.*

In its most essential form, the "contract" sets each of us marching to our own drummer. We use its cadence to set our life rhythms and to give us direction. Our drummer echoes our heartbeat, reminding us who we truly are, about our own values, ethics and aesthetics.

But who is our drummer? What is our contract? The answer is different for each of us. And being honest with ourselves can be a difficult, lifelong process of searching for ever-deepening awareness. It's bringing our unconscious selves—our hidden desires, feelings, fears, thoughts—to consciousness so that they can be understood. Without a clear look at our internal truths, our unconscious self is running the show. We can't explain some of our choices because we're driven by things we don't fully understand.

This becomes an awesome task because very often the essential truth is not always apparent. The trip into our subconscious may be painful or require action that we don't want to take, but it is critical in helping to make us emotionally healthy, indeed happy.

The Crabapple Tree

Truth to self is very much like the extensive root system of the crabapple, a tree named for its sour fruit but celebrated for its beautiful blossoms, strength and longevity. This kind of truth is invisible, known only to ourselves, in the same way that the root system of the tree is invisible.

Though they're buried deep in the earth, the roots keep the tree sound. The deeper and better spread they are, the more likely is the tree to withstand the forces that work against it. It will survive environmental pressures—drought, wind, pollution and extreme temperatures. And the hearty, invisible roots will feed the tree as they hold it stable. It will flower beautifully, its leaves will be lush and verdant and its fruit will be plentiful.

Likewise, truth to ourselves is a hidden conversation, a private truth we need if we wish to be ultimately happy. With an extensive root system of internal truth-telling, we are like the crabapple. We are more grounded and can better withstand outside forces such as emotional storms, attack from others and pressures to be persuaded to do things that aren't good for us. We're also healthy enough to fend off the pollution of information overload. We are stable. The deep-buried roots of truth nourish our souls as they make our relationships flower.

Truth is tough. It will not break, like a bubble, at a
touch, nay, you may kick it about all day like a football,
and it will be round and full at evening.

Oliver Wendell Holmes, The Professor at the Breakfast Table

These are the classic questions: What is the price of truth? Would we violate our internal truths to have more money? What if we really needed the money? In the next story, Elena really needed the money.

$20,000 and the Truth

Elena is a housemaid who lives at the poverty line in an urban *barrio,* with her husband and three teenage sons. In spite of her poverty, her dream has been to send her children to college. Working double shifts, she has been able to put away a few dollars each month. Elena was hired for her present position five years ago—the consequence of circumstances that impressed her employer, Mrs. Frost.

Elena had worked as a maid for Mrs. Frost's elderly neighbor, Mrs. Rosen, a retired bookkeeper. On the day Mrs. Rosen died, Elena called Mrs. Frost to the apartment. Elena told Mrs. Frost that she wanted to show her something before calling the authorities.

Elena took me into the bedroom. There she reached to the back of a dresser drawer which held stacks of money—later determined to be over $20,000. Elena was afraid the police might confiscate the money so she asked me to call Mrs. Rosen's sister.

When the sister arrived she was astonished. She had no idea the cash was there. Even more amazing to me was that it hadn't occurred to Elena to take the money for herself, even though it would not have been missed by any of us. I hired Elena the next day.

To Elena, truth has no price. The fact that Mrs. Rosen's savings could have meant the difference between poverty and greatly improved circumstances made no difference to her. Elena told us:

Happiness is not money. Worrying about not having enough, being in debt makes me unhappy. But I also know that having money is not what makes me happy.

What makes me happy is the time I spend with my family, my church, friends. It doesn't matter, rich or poor, I would still do these things. With more money I would not worry so much. But nothing is greater to me than my feelings about myself. Feeling proud about the way I live my life is what makes me happy.

This is an example of the contract in full operation. Elena has clarity about her own needs. Her primary need is to be truthful with herself. Her unwavering honesty is the source of her happiness. Regardless of her economic stresses, she has achieved something that many far richer people have not: She lives happily with herself.

It is necessary to the happiness of man that
he be mentally faithful to himself.

Thomas Paine

Finding Your Own Truth

The following exercise is a variation of an activity we do during the workshops. It is an opportunity to uncover your own truths.

Find a time when you can be alone. Place yourself close to a mirror and look yourself in the eyes. Complete both of the following phrases:

"I pretend that _____."

"The truth is _____."

Keep repeating the phrases and filling in the blanks as you face yourself. Remember that you're not looking for fantasies like "I pretend I won the lottery." You're looking for things you really pretend to yourself: "I pretend that I have a close relationship with my sister." And, "The truth is, I don't share most of my feelings with her."

Since you are alone in the room, there is no risk of exposure. It has been our experience that, if you continue to fill in the blanks, you will discover things about yourself of which you are not currently aware. Deeply held secrets and truths may begin to surface in your own mind.

We have found that everyone pretends something. Bringing these things into a conscious arena, particularly in a private environment, is a wonderful technique for encountering your true self.

This is an exercise you can do regularly or when you need some clarification.

A variation of the exercise can be done with someone you trust, a loved one: Face your partner. Alternate completing the two statements above. As your partner speaks, you might try taking down notes. After about ten minutes, you can break the cycle and "debrief." You might consider the following:

What have I learned about myself? My partner?

Am I surprised by what I heard from my partner?

Were there any major revelations?

What were the themes we expressed? How do these themes relate to real issues in our lives?

How did it feel to encounter my own truths? My partner's truths?

This Marriage Is Over!

You may remember Annie's story about dinner party leftovers from Chapter 8. At about the same time Annie was re-evaluating her childhood training about "giving," she was also struggling with the truth about her real feelings, especially in relation to her husband Bruce. Like other women of her generation, Annie, now sixty, married for the first time right out of college and had three children by the time she was twenty-five.

I wasn't happy at the time but I kept telling myself that I soon would be—as soon as my husband got out of med school or as soon as we had a real home, and on and on. Over time all of these things came to pass but I still felt empty.

It took me a long time to realize that overcoming my unhappiness required that I become honest with myself. Being honest about my real needs was a very difficult thing to do. I hadn't been brought up that way. In spite of the wonderful parts

of my life, there was something very much out of kilter—my
marriage. And I was lying to myself about it.

To Annie, even identifying her own needs was a revolutionary activity. As a first step she had to buck social pressure to discover what she valued in herself. After a lot of self-evaluation she concluded that there were many things she loved about herself—particularly her creativity and ingenuity.

Unfortunately, these were not qualities her husband valued in her. As time passed she began to feel completely misunderstood by him. Her greatest values were secrets she felt she couldn't share.

I remember one disastrous night—Fourth of July, 1966. The
reason I remember the exact date is that it was a pivotal night in
my life. After a backyard barbecue, I decided to do something
special before the kids' bedtime. To dramatize a fairy tale, I
pulled my lacy wedding dress down from the closet and put it on
with the veil, the shoes, the whole bit. Then I danced around the
living room pretending to be a fairy princess. It was all in good
fun and the kids loved it.

But my husband got sarcastic and hostile. He attacked my
fantasy world and put me down in front of the kids. I felt so
ashamed.

That night, I realized I was doing some pretending of my
own. Bruce had been blasting the parts of me that I cherished the
most. But I had created my own fairy tale out of desperation—
that I was in love with my handsome husband, that I was happy
spending time with him and that I didn't need anything else in
my life. These were all myths I told myself about myself. These
were easy myths to keep alive. I was believing everything that
mothers in the 1960s were supposed to believe. By repeating
them over and over to my family and friends I believed them
wholeheartedly myself.

What I discovered were two important truths: My husband

*had no interest in ever knowing the real me. And I had to leave
this marriage.*

*When people found out that I was planning to leave my
husband, they suggested all sorts of dishonest ploys to allow me
to stay married. I was told, "Just buck up—you don't have to
indulge your feelings," or "Couldn't you just have a discreet little
affair?" These people who supposedly loved me told me to live a
lie just to keep up appearances.*

*But by this time I was clear. I needed to live a life where I
could be me. As terrible as divorce is to children, I believe it is
most important to be a parental role model. The message I most
wanted to give my kids is:* You don't need to live a lie.

After the divorce, Annie fell in love with Paul, with whom she
has been happily married for more than thirty years. Together they
have five grown children. She continues to value her creativity and
imagination. Annie currently serves as a master teacher of high school
literature, leads a renowned creative-writing project and has flourished as a talented short-story writer.

*I know what's true for me . . . and that's enough. I don't need
anything else. I believe self-understanding is the most important
ingredient of happiness. When I just stay true to myself I'm
happy. If all my decisions are filtered through this sense of truth,
I can't go wrong!*

It is only when we pull back the layers of pretense that keep personal myths alive that we can tell the truth as we see it. Without the
overlays of self-deception our vision of ourselves comes clear. We call
this "my truth."

The great enemy of the truth is very often not the lie—
deliberate, contrived, and dishonest—but the myth—
persistent, persuasive, and unrealistic.

John F. Kennedy, at Yale University, 1962

"My Truth"

You can envision the concept of "my truth" if you imagine that each of us is a camera that sees the world through a slightly different lens and angle. The lens is affected by our background, culture, life experience and genetics. It is also mediated by our emotional framework and the degree to which we are invested in the event we're viewing. Though we're looking at the same scene, our image of that scene— our "truth"—is at least slightly different from anyone else's. Sometimes it's vastly different.

Imagine an extended family, the perfect environment to see the phenomenon of "my truth" in full flower. The family is sitting at the Thanksgiving table. Over pumpkin pie, Uncle Joe and Uncle Don start arguing vociferously about a joint business deal that went bad twenty years ago.

If you were to poll the other nine people sitting around the table, you'd find that, even though they witnessed the exact same argument, each had a different story, or "truth," about what happened between the two men at the table. So, what is the real "truth"?

Aunt Rose, Uncle Joe's wife, has a sad "camera lens" because she's lived for two decades with the loss of their nest egg. She thinks it's Don's fault because he made the bad investment, and, in her mind, he started the fight tonight. On the other hand, Great-Aunt Ida is well off, so the money angle is of no interest to her. She sees the fight as completely childish. Cousin Bob, a therapist, thinks it's healthy for men to express their emotions openly. Lynette, a mother of two and an in-law, is appalled, because her own family would never air its dirty laundry like this. Seven-year-old Melissa thinks the whole thing is funny, while younger sister Madeline is frightened. So who's right? They are all right. Each reaction is honest and valid.

We can never be wrong with our truth, because the viewing lens is uniquely ours. The best we can do is to tell our truth honestly and to allow others to do the same. If this family endeavored to find an objective truth, they would waste a great deal of time. Undertaking the impossible task of assigning right and wrong could lead to a division into camps, misunderstandings and alienation—in short, a polarized family.

By contrast, allowing each person to have their own truth leads to a unified family that encourages a diversity of viewpoints. This creates a gentle, accepting and happier group.

The Truth About What You Need

How do you feel when you express your truths to family and friends? What happens to you emotionally when you make honest demands at work? Do you hear a little voice that whispers "shoulds" in your ear: "You shouldn't be so pushy. You shouldn't express your needs. You should be satisfied with what you have." Maybe sometimes that little voice isn't a whisper, it's a roar.

Dancing with the Deadly "Shoulds"

We've all danced with the "shoulds"—the persistent requirement by our families, friends and communities that we need what they need, live as they live, believe as they believe and express ourselves in ways they think we should. Whether the "shoulds" come from the loving heart of our mother, the pulpit or the political process, they are delivered from the outside—external demands that may be in direct opposition to personal truth. If we allow the "shoulds" to overshadow our needs, we are allowing ourselves to violate our personal contracts.

Sixteen-year-old Shana was named the happiest person at her Atlanta-area high school. When we did an informal poll of her friends they agreed. She's resilient, smart and funny.

> If a situation crops up that I'm not sure of, I stop dead in my tracks and I really think about it. What do I really believe? What do I honestly want? And sometimes that's quite different from what's expected of me by my friends or family. If I don't take time to analyze, I get off track. I want to be truthful to myself instead of saying things just because I think I'll get everyone else's approval. It makes me happier than just about anything else.

We interviewed Shana in her home and talked with her family afterward. There is tension in the household. Shana is seen as selfish and socially unacceptable by her stepmother, Connie.

> Oh, she's honest all right, but at the expense of others. I think Shana's a selfish child. For example, when she has friends over they check the refrigerator for snacks. Shana asks them what they want to eat and tells them what she wants to eat, too! That is not polite. She should wait for them first.
>
> "Other people first," I always say. That's why when my son, Joey, and I are looking in the fridge for something to eat, neither one of us will go first. He's so generous he's almost afraid to say what he wants. If he ends up with my preference, I feel that I've done the right thing.

What seems like an almost insignificant example becomes an important glimpse into how this family feels about truth. The difference in their approach damages this parent-child relationship. Connie truly believes that expressing her own needs is selfish, while denying her needs is generous.

Connie grew up with the "shoulds" that many of us have been

taught: She *should* be a sacrificing mother and put her children's needs first; she *should* defer to others; and she *should* teach her son to put others' needs before his own. They become rules that Connie creates to determine how she should act, feel or be in order to gain acceptance and feel good about herself. But here's the problem: Even though her behavior is culturally acceptable, it makes her fundamentally dishonest to herself and others.

Connie is not happy and told us that she scoffs at the idea that happiness is possible. Her "shoulds" are the source of her unhappiness. Why? Let's compare Shana's approach with Connie's:

• Shana meets her own needs by interacting honestly with people. Connie often doesn't get what she wants, walking away from interactions feeling deprived.

• By her own example, Shana clearly encourages her friends to meet their own needs. Connie is unclear with Joey, so he can't evaluate her needs and feels hesitant to assert his own.

• Shana empowers her friends to match her honesty with their own. Connie is teaching Joey to deny his needs, ironically, by being dishonest with himself and with Connie.

• When Shana interacts with people, everybody gets what they want or walks away with an openly negotiated settlement. Since Connie believes that asserting her own needs is selfish, it is inevitable that her son—or anyone else who negotiates with her—will walk away feeling guilty. Perhaps he inadvertently took something she wanted? He'll never know.

It's interesting to note that Shana is one of the most well-liked teenagers in her school. Her peers describe her as generous and friendly. Rather than being put off by her, they can rely on her for honest feedback. They don't have to guess what she wants, and her behavior enables her friends to express their own needs openly.

Connie, on the other hand, was described by one acquaintance as being "emotionally opaque and withholding." Because she doesn't give her friends an honest "read" on her needs and reactions she seems emotionally unavailable. Her silence is dishonest and becomes an obstacle to establishing intimacy with people she cares about.

So what can Connie do? Is there a quick fix? If we look carefully at happy people we see a process of self-analysis that leads to self-awareness. Connie might consider asking herself the following questions:

• How did I learn the "shoulds" that govern my life?

• What "shoulds" drive my behavior?

• What are my fears about being honest? What will I lose if I am honest?

• How can I honestly express my needs and encourage Joey to express his, too?

Big Truths and Little White Lies

Truth is like a crossword puzzle. If one small word is incorrect, you have to manipulate all of the words around that one inaccuracy to complete the puzzle. This is why even "little white lies" are stressful. We have to remember the lie and who we told it to. We have to worry about being caught or that someone will expose us. But most of all, like the word in the puzzle, we are out of alignment with what we know is true.

This is why Leticia gave them up years ago when she opened her art gallery. She only had two choices: either tell the artists little white lies to "let them down easy" or give them honest feedback with the intention of improving their art. She decided to tell the truth, and she did not hold back.

As a result, a wonderful thing happened. Because she enforced her own code of honesty, an ever-growing circle of artists began to trust her. In fact, she became a touchstone for artists all over the Midwest, who came to her specifically for her reactions. In Leticia they had found someone who cared enough to risk the truth.

With a wry laugh, Leticia told us that she hasn't lied for years—even to a close friend with a terrible hairdo.

> *I believe that I never do someone a service by telling them anything that isn't true. I don't distinguish between little lies about clothes or recipes and big lies about ethics or money. Truth is truth. Even if it doesn't initially seem positive, it is real.*
>
> *There is a huge benefit for me in being truthful to others. In the long run it deepens my relationships. I don't have any halfway friends. They rely on me, I rely on them. The substance of our friendship is honesty. Can you imagine anything more comforting or more inviting?*

But Leticia found herself in a situation that tested her resolve.

Leticia does volunteer work at a health center, where she works one-on-one with AIDS patients. Two years ago she was assigned to Jean. They hit it off immediately and Leticia found herself devoting every Saturday to Jean.

The two women were fond of each other, yet Leticia eventually became uncomfortable with Jean's growing dependence on her. She found herself in the difficult situation of having to be honest about her own needs in spite of Jean's illness.

> *I felt Jean's requests for favors were beginning to snowball out of control. I found myself beginning to respond to her out of duty rather than desire. But I was particularly torn because Jean's illness was getting worse.*
>
> *I could have fabricated a story about why I couldn't spend as much time with her—"My brother's in town this weekend,"*

et cetera. But I wanted to respect my relationship with Jean. So I had a long talk with her about exactly how I was feeling. And I asked her to tell me how she was feeling. We brainstormed together—her needs, my needs, how could we meet each other's needs and look for additional resources for Jean.

The conversation was difficult and a little scary at first. We both had to be extremely honest. And we did work things out. Jean was very candid with me. Some of her needs simply couldn't be met, but most we could deal with. In the end we both felt a tremendous sense of loving toward one another.

How can we turn down the requests of a person with AIDS? What kind of selfish people are we to assert our needs when someone else is ill or disabled or needy? Many of us assume that being a "good person" means putting aside our own interests in favor of the interests of someone who is less fortunate. Isn't that what we *should* do?

By denying our own needs we are being dishonest with ourselves. But our needs and the needs of others are not mutually exclusive. Leticia's truth brought about greater clarity for Jean. She was able to be truthful to herself while lovingly extending herself to Jean. When we are truthful we empower others to be truthful in return and we have a far greater chance of meeting everyone's needs.

Accountable Truth-telling

The word *truth* can be terribly abused. We've all seen it used as a weapon. People who use personal attack masquerading as "just telling the truth" will often say, "I'm very honest. I just tell it the way it is." But under the guise of honesty, that statement translates into the license to say, "It's your fault." "You blew it." Or "Honestly, you're a jerk." Accountable truth-telling has nothing to do with blame.

Happy people view truth as something precious, and they nurture it carefully. Using truth as a tool to hurt someone, or to abuse a truth in any way, would not only be unaccountable but also intolerable.

To Leticia, being true to herself does not mean indiscriminate truth-telling. Leticia's intention is not to punish, hurt or attack. She didn't set out to be judgmental or personally critical. Her conversation didn't start with "Jean, you're being selfish. You're demanding too much of my time." Rather, Leticia approached Jean compassionately and with the intention of sharing her own feelings about herself and what she was experiencing. We can only find real truth when we move away from our judgments of others and start paying attention to our own behavior and needs.

He offends no one.
Yet he speaks the truth.
His words are clear
But never harsh.

The Dhammapada, *from "The True Master"*

Confronting the Pink Elephant

The "Pink Elephant" is the family beast that no one will talk about. It gets its power from dishonesty. No one will recognize its existence so it runs amok. Families keep it alive so that they won't have to deal openly with pain. The symbolic elephant might be an unacknowledged addiction to drugs and alcohol or the physical abuse of children. It may be a secret illness or the sadness of a family tragedy that has gone ungrieved. Regardless of its cause, the Pink Elephant lumbers through the home with disastrous effect, pushing aside honest emotions as it crushes the lives of the family.

Clint, now forty-six, grew up in the rolling hills of Virginia. By all appearances he had an idyllic childhood—a beautiful home in a community of Victorian houses with a classic Main Street surrounded by green parklands. The annual Christmas photo depicted a wholesome American family of the 1950s. But a Pink Elephant was ruining their lives:

> When I was very young I remember saying to my father, "I think Mom is drinking too much." Each time he would tell me I was wrong and that she was just feeling stressed or tired. But I could see it for myself. Mom would be crying and slurring her speech when I got home from school. She could barely stand up, let alone cook dinner for us. Dad made it clear, however, that we didn't talk about it. Whenever I pushed him for answers, he'd withdraw from me.
>
> All of this had a terrible effect on me. After awhile I questioned my own intuitions and reactions. This was my father, after all, and he was the adult. Maybe there was something wrong with me.

Clint was told by the responsible adults in his life that his perceptions were wrong. Eventually, he felt he couldn't trust his own ability to reason. Even when he knew his analysis was true, he chose to lie to himself and his family so that he could continue to receive love from them. There were clear-cut rewards for going along with the family mythology. Clint was being crushed by the Pink Elephant.

> I was stuck in a trap. If I told the truth my father wouldn't love me. If I lied I couldn't love myself. I may not have seen it clearly back then, but my mother's inability to function was much less of a problem than the frustration and anger I felt at not being able to talk about it.

Clint's fury and outrage drove him away from the family as a teenager. He felt alienated from his parents.

> When I went away to college I realized that the lies were deeply rooted in me and were a tremendously destructive power in my

life. I couldn't even make close contact with my roommate,
because I felt I had to hide the family lie.

I knew that if I wanted to be happy I had to break my
pattern and get at the truth. Ultimately, the lie kept me from
happiness—it did nothing to protect me. In fact it only
negatively affected the people around me, and ended up
hurting me the most.

In his early twenties, Clint began a search for his own truths. He
focused on the hurt and anguish he had grown up with. He realized
he had internalized the Pink Elephant—not only would he avoid talking about his mother's alcoholism, he couldn't talk about anything
difficult. Inside he was seething. He knew he needed help. Finally,
working with a therapist, he was able to let the rage out. That was the
beginning of a new way of life.

For years, Clint has maintained a commitment to the truth.
Even in times of tragedy, this has served him well. Several years ago,
Clint learned that his father was dying. He knew this was his last
chance to share "His Truth" with his father. He flew home to
Virginia.

The conversation was cathartic and transforming. Even though
his dad's perception of what had happened years ago was very different from his own, Clint came to understand more about his childhood through the eyes of his father.

It was one of the most important things I ever did. It wasn't that
I needed him to see it my way. I just needed him to know what
was going on inside my head at the time—to share myself with
him. He died three weeks later.

I have a rule: If I'm afraid to say it, then I force myself to say
it. If I'm afraid to feel it, I force myself to feel it. It's only in the
past few years that I've developed the confidence to understand
and trust myself. I am the only person who knows the answer.

I'm the only one who knows what's true for me. If I want to be
happy, I have to tell my truth.

A personal truth is a truth is a truth. It can't be garnished, dis-
guised or changed. It just is what it is. And it emerges with great clarity when we drop the dishonesty that obscures it.

When truth is buried, it grows, it chokes, it gathers
such explosive force that on the day it breaks
out it blows everything up with it.

Emile Zola, "J'Accuse," L'Aurore, 1898

Whether it's deflating the Pink Elephant, setting the record
straight or sharing an unstated feeling like love, the act of telling the
truth corrects what can become a poisonous situation. Truth-telling
is a loving thing to do. Even if we don't always say it perfectly, it affirms our willingness to honor the importance of our relationships.

Tom: A "Coming Out" Story

"Coming out"—telling the world that you are homosexual—has become a modern archetype for the most far-reaching kind of honesty.
This process requires truth on many levels with many people. It involves, first, coming to terms with one's self and then honestly com-
municating to others—family, friends, coworkers and the community
at large.

Coming out often takes place in a culture that finds homosex-
uality deplorable. It can be emotionally wrenching and sometimes ex-
poses the individual to physical violence.

So why risk it? Because it is the essence of truth-telling.

I was very much in the closet. I was a gay man working for a
sporting-goods manufacturer—part of the company's macho

athletic culture. This was a back-slapping, locker room kind of
place. Frankly, I resented that telling the truth meant discussing
my sex life. I felt uncomfortable about being gay in this work
environment.

So I hid my life. I hid my vacation pictures. I referred to my
partner of ten years as my girlfriend, and lived in fear that
someone from the office would see Jon and me together on the
streets.

Tom's lie was taking a toll. But Tom felt his livelihood was de-
pendent on his high-powered marketing job. He had just purchased
a new house with a hefty mortgage and booked a cruise to Mexico. He
drove a nice car and maintained a high standard of living. Somehow,
though, none of this seemed to be right. Along with the stress of his
secret life came health issues. Tom was diagnosed with ulcers.

I tried everything. Medication, meditation, you name it. I even
bought a Japanese worry stone hoping it would help. On paper I
had such a wonderful life—loving relationship, wonderful
friends, plenty of money. But I was miserable.

One day in desperation Tom confided to a coworker that he was
gay. And in the following weeks his worst fears came true. As gossip
started to fly, people began to talk behind his back and make jokes
about him. Some of his fellow workers withdrew from him altogether.
He had the impression that his upward career path was suddenly derailed. The life he had valued was beginning to unravel.

Strangely, though, he felt better. Then the light bulb went on.
The issue was that he'd not only been dishonest with others, it was
that he had been dishonest with himself. He had convinced himself
that he would be able to hide out for the rest of his life.

Within a week I quit my job and felt great. The stress left my
body. I could tell the truth about myself. I could be who I was. I
still had the big mortgage but suddenly I was stronger. I began to

like myself for the first time in years. And now, all of a sudden there seemed to be so many possibilities for me.

The most immediate impact was on my relationship with Jon. I was actively affirming my love for him by accepting myself. All of the wonderful parts of my life were suddenly real. Being me meant I could enjoy all of it.

Truthfulness had liberated me. When I thought about my next job, instead of focusing on how much money I could make or prestige and title, I honestly looked at my passions.

Once he focused his job search, Tom was quickly hired as a production assistant for the biggest theater company in town.

I had a job in my favorite field! I had loved theater since I was five years old and saw my first show. Even though my salary was cut in half, I felt indestructible. My truth was my power. Truth had been the missing link in my life.

Then I started to "come out" to everyone. I was surprised by what happened. I was worried I'd lose family and friends. In fact, the opposite happened—people were drawn to me. The secrecy disappeared, and the discomfort people felt around me disappeared with it. In the couple of cases where people did pull away, I was ready to deal with the consequences.

People are drawn to the truth. They want the truth. It's like a magnet. They are attracted to those who are honest. As we heard more and more stories that illustrate how honesty invites intimacy, we began to refer to this phenomenon as "the truth magnet."

As I told my story to the world, I got back stories that were astounding. I think by being so open, it gave other people permission to be more open with me. For almost every person I told my story, I'd hear a story from them about something hidden in their past, or secret desires, sadness, joys, fears that seemed much more private and personal than my own.

My intimate relationships with dozens of people have deepened beyond anything I might have imagined. I have relationships that are honest and true with people on whom I can really rely. I've gotten closer to my family, closer to my friends, and my partnership with Jon has gotten better and better—mostly because my own stress level has gone down. I'm now a volunteer working to support gay teens.

Withholding a truth that is so much an intimate part of who we are can have far-reaching effects. It can cause tension in the body, distancing of relationships, lack of motivation, burnout, fatigue and illness. During our interview with Tom he told us he'd experienced all of these things.

Tom is now the head of marketing for the theater company. He works closely with some of the people and on some of the plays he has most admired since childhood. He still keeps the worry stone on his nightstand as a reminder that he never wants to be in that "awful, secretive place again."

When one is pretending, the entire body revolts.

Anaïs Nin

Like Pebbles in a Clear Lake

To Chay Ky, a master car mechanic, honesty is the fundamental element in his deeply spiritual approach to life. This gentle man survived the political horrors of his native Cambodia with his deep happiness intact. Chay's view of honesty is rock solid. Clearly his dedication to truthfulness was an element in his survival and later successes.

Chay's profession is not known for honest practitioners. He told us about his relationship with his customers.

I never lie to my clients. Heaven and Hell don't happen when you die. They happen as you live. Lying is Hell; truth is Heaven.

I prefer to live in Heaven. My customers know this about me,
and they keep coming back.

   Truth is the only thing that brings inner harmony. Without
truth, nothing matters. But when I find it I am truly happy. And
I will spend a wondrous lifetime searching for truth. Truth is as
apparent in a diseased refugee camp as it is in a modern city.

   In this search I have learned that truth is happiness—it exists
simply and cannot be changed. What is wonderful is that
untruths can *be changed for the better—they* can *be changed*
into truths. You are never lost for truth as long as you search for
truth.

   Truth is seeing the pebbles at the bottom of a lake. I know
I've found truth when the water clears, and the shapes on the
bottom are sharp and colorful. There is no question when I see
the truth. . . .

The truth shall make you free.

John 8:32

Does the wheel end at truthfulness, our last of the nine choices?
No. As with any circle, this is only one segment in an ever-moving design. As giving has flowed into this segment, truthfulness now flows
back to accountability. Because, after all, how can you be fully accountable to yourself unless you know your truth?

Once again, all of the choices are driven by intention. What is
our intention when we're dealing with ourselves and others? Is it to
hide, to protect, to hurt, to manipulate, to punish, or is it to enlighten,
to help, to be authentic and genuine?

We continue to move around the wheel, as the adventure of
ever-increasing contentment, centeredness and capability continues.
We are on a lifelong journey when we choose to be happy.

Chapter 10

Synergy

Appreciation → Giving → Truthfulness → Accountability → Identification → Centrality → Recasting → Options →

Intention

You have now experienced each of the nine choices individually. It's time to bring them together as they truly are—parts of a self-regulating, synergistic system.

If we may indulge in the world of metaphors and symbols one last time, we find that the solar system, with its ever-spinning planets revolving around the sun, is our most descriptive model for happiness. Like the sun, intention is at the center of this constantly moving system, always driving the other eight choices with its energy and keeping them in alignment with the strength of its gravity. And the eight choices, each one a viable world of its own, add profoundly to the energy and gravitational forces that keep the individual planets in their own orbits and the entire system unified. Because of the synergy between the planets and their sun, our small corner of the universe neither collapses in on itself nor flies apart. In much the same way, the nine choices exert force on one another to keep the system whole.

This balancing force within the system is most apparent when any one of the choices becomes inactive. For example, our intention to be happy would lose its momentum if identification stopped providing information on what would, indeed, make us happy. Giving would run amok; we'd give away everything we have without the moderating forces of accountability and truthfulness to self to keep it in balance. And recasting would become virtually useless without our choice to open new options and possibilities.

If we follow the solar system metaphor a bit further, we begin to see the system of nine choices as part of a much larger set of experiential, emotional and physiological galaxies. This is a complex universe of systems that all interact and, in fact, are all components of a far greater whole—the whole self.

These systems are many. Moving through space and interacting with the nine choices are the recently discovered contributions to happiness of biochemistry and genetics. Our physical environment and world ecology also exert force on our choices as do our constellations of belief, experience and spirituality. Our systems of cultural memory, philosophy, politics and ideology all work to make our choices personal and singular. And as we begin to understand the nuances of the components that make up a complete person, we begin to comprehend and appreciate what makes us unique, happy individuals.

Of necessity, we have spent a great deal of time understanding each of the nine choices. But what does it look like when this entire planetary system is flourishing? What happens to people when all the choices are up and running? As you will see in our final stories, regardless of how difficult life circumstances may be, these choices come together to create a cohesive system. Their synergy generates the feeling of happiness, the warm glow and calm of extremely happy people.

Two Happy Lives

We've saved two stories for last. Both illustrate this synergy. We could have picked from any of the hundreds of people we interviewed, each of whom has stories that integrate the happiness choices in coordinated action. First, we chose Kathryn, someone you met in the Prologue and have followed throughout the book. And, second, we chose Hiroshi, from Chapter 8 ("Giving"), whose participation in the "commerce of giving" resulted in the education of hundreds of employees from his carpet-cleaning business.

In both cases, the stories you're about to read took place more than a year after our initial interviews.

Kathryn's Story—Part Four

Kathryn is a wonderful example of someone who made the transition from unhappy to happy as an adult. As you recall, she learned it on her own—every move was conscious and deliberate.

When you visit Kathryn's ballroom you can't miss the large sign posted above the entrance: "This Is a Place to Experience Joy." With a staff of thirty, and over five hundred customers per week, she manages a large operation. What guides her?

> *My purpose each day and what drives each decision is to live as happily as I can and provide an opportunity for others to do the same. Because my life used to be so joyless, joy is now the center of everything for me.*

Recently Kathryn came up against a serious roadblock. Here's the story and how she dealt with it:

Kathryn's ballroom was thriving. At forty-seven, she was beating the odds and was about to realize another dream—becoming a national ballroom dance champion. After years of intensive training, she and her partner, Michael, were at their peak. They now moved in perfect unison, rehearsed well together, and seemed to be unstoppable. They had become real artists, mixing technical excellence with an unusual ability to convey emotion, beauty and grace on the dance floor. They were beginning to place in the top ten in national competitions.

But one day Michael dropped a bombshell. He announced he was leaving Kathryn to take on a new partner, Mae, an instructor who worked in the ballroom.

> It was a blow. My last chance to realize a dream had vanished. I had to face the reality of the situation. At my age there was no hope I could start over with a new partner.

Kathryn entered the beginning of the *recasting* process. For forty-eight hours she felt physically ill from the loss and grief—almost like a flu. She let herself have the physical experience until she was done.

As her grief ebbed, Kathryn began looking for meaning. Ultimately, she learned many lessons—about partnership, about her own ability to commit long-term, about interpersonal contracts and about assumptions. This experience also provided an opportunity for her to reflect on her love of dance and the role of competition in her life.

She started to sort things out. What were her *intentions*? Were they to blame herself? Punish Michael and Mae? Get revenge? Kick both of them out of the studio?

She knew almost from the start that her intention was to emerge from this happily and to keep the toxicity of the event from affecting her choices. This led her directly to personal *accountability*. She committed to making the situation the best it could be. Blaming Michael, Mae or herself wouldn't work at all.

Kathryn began to *identify* what would work best under the circumstances. The following Monday morning, she approached Michael and Mae. She told them her feelings and, at the same time, pledged her full support. She offered them use of the studio whenever they wanted and reassured them that their jobs at the ballroom would remain secure. She gave them her blessing. She emerged from the conversation with two potential dance champions who considered her a great friend and remained committed to her ballroom.

As a guide to where to go next, Kathryn came back to her *centrality*—dance, pure and simple, without the taint of blame, disappointment or unhappiness. With dance as her motivator she began to consider her *options*. What were the opportunities?

> *I now had a lot of time that was previously devoted to rehearsal and competition. I decided to use it to realize another dream— opening up a second studio—a chance to increase the business and offer new specialty classes. I don't see limitations. They don't exist for me anymore. I focus on what is and what could be. Whenever there's change I say, "OK, what's new for me now?"*

By opening the new studio, Kathryn enabled herself to do something important, something she loved.

> *I learned a long time ago that one of my greatest satisfactions is sharing 100 percent of my knowledge. I want to be the best teacher, no matter what I'm teaching. At the new studio, I have a whole new opportunity to teach master classes and develop people whose goal is the same as mine was twenty years ago: to be a dance instructor.*
>
> *Giving is habit-forming. I don't give to get, but getting is invariably what happens.*

Kathryn was replacing her feelings of disappointment and hurt with an emerging sense of *appreciation*. Though her career as a competition dancer had been derailed, she was thriving with a second smaller ballroom down the street and a chance to provide a diversity of dance parties and classes. Her staff, including Michael and Mae, were cohesive and more dedicated than ever.

Finally, *truthfulness* about herself became the lens through which Kathryn evaluated what had happened. Her reactions to the situation were authentic and honest. She's had to face up to some hard lessons. She has accepted that her days in competition are over—the dream of winning a national championship will never be accomplished. She has had to take a critical look at her mistakes when she originally forged the dance partnership with Michael.

Kathryn has learned a lot in the more than forty years we've chronicled throughout the book. She has learned each of the nine choices on her own. Today she lives each day feeling fully alive. She is happy.

Hiroshi

Hiroshi didn't tell us at the time of our first interview that he was in the fifth year of remission from lymphoma. Without ever mentioning his current health, Hiroshi had openly recounted living through the anti-Japanese prejudice of his childhood and his business successes. His stories of personal generosity and mentoring exemplified the "commerce of giving."

One year after our initial interview Hiroshi saw his doctor for a routine physical. The results were poor—Hiroshi's lymphoma had recurred. Oncologists confirmed that Hiroshi had no more than nine months to live.

With his customary giving, Hiroshi generously gave us an opportunity, through interviews, to understand how the nine choices of

happy people work during the most difficult times. Some of this insight comes directly from Hiroshi, and some from his daughter, who
visited the doctors with him.

When Hiroshi first received the news, he hung his head in shock. He
sat, shoulders hunched, silently looking at the floor. After a pause, he
dropped his shoulders and looked squarely at the doctor.

> *I've been happy during my time to live. Now I have a time to die.*
> *Between now and then, I will live even more.*

Hiroshi's *intention* to live richly was matched by his *accountability*. He drilled the doctor for information about his future capabilities—would he be able to travel, would he be in pain, what would
his medical needs be?

Once he established the parameters of his future, Hiroshi committed himself to a course of action. His sense of personal accountability pushed him to create the best future possible under trying
circumstances. Using *identification* he made a list of all the things he
wanted to do in the next nine months.

> *My time is limited. I must do the things that are most important*
> *to me. I will visit my sister in Chicago. I will spend deep time*
> *with my wife and daughter. I will contact all my relatives and*
> *close friends to say proper good-byes. And I must leave*
> *instructions so that my assets are properly used to educate others.*

Faced with a finite time on earth, Hiroshi began to *centralize* his
list. He began traveling for his last meetings. He contacted friends
and relatives, and he made his final wishes known to his family.

Hiroshi had spent years quietly considering his own mortality.
In a sense, he had *recast* his own death in advance. He understood
its finality and had embraced the notion of a "physical ending"
as "completion"—something of beauty. He had balanced his sadness at leaving earth with a feeling that his life had been rich and

important—that he had given of himself freely to others. He saw himself as one person departing, with many people staying behind who carried him in their souls.

With a short time to live, Hiroshi was still opening *options* and thinking divergently. How would he die? He didn't know and couldn't plan it accurately. So he threw out the net.

> *I have found many ways to die. I might go in a hospice. Or I am prepared for a long stay in the hospital. I may be lucky to stay at home in my own bed. I have also considered an assisted death, if I am in pain. I am lucky to have so many choices. . . .*

Hiroshi continued to show his *appreciation* of the world through his characteristic *giving*. After first being sure that his family was adequately protected, Hiroshi wrote a will leaving all his remaining assets to an educational trust to be administered by his daughter. His father's gift from the 1930s—the promise that he would seek wisdom—would be passed to another generation.

And finally, Hiroshi has told himself and everyone around him the *truth*.

> *The only big lie I could tell is to deny I am dying. And that's ridiculous. Death is as true as you can get. Now having said that, is there anything else to hide? Is there any reason to lie? Being honest about my death makes me even more honest about my life.*

Are you wondering why Hiroshi isn't afraid of dying? He expressed no fear, either during our interviews or to any family member.

If fear is actually the fear of being unable to cope, Hiroshi wouldn't be afraid of death itself. He would be afraid of being unable to cope with death. It is clear that his use of the nine choices has given him the ability to do just that.

It may seem oxymoronic, but Hiroshi is living his final months in deep happiness. He is living his life with feelings of capability, cen-teredness and contentment. Is he sad about his impending death? Yes. Is he happy about his long and meaningful life? Yes. His rich pic-ture of life is of an entire glass—partially empty and partially full.

What could be better than looking back on a life filled with such joy. And I intend to be joyful every day, to my best ability, even in this final process.

I do not know it . . .

It is without name . . .

It is a word unsaid,

it is not in any dictionary or utterance or symbol . . .

It is not chaos or death . . .

It is a form and union and plan . . .

It is eternal life . . .

It is happiness.

Walt Whitman, from Leaves of Grass, 1856

Afterword

With the publication of *How We Choose to Be Happy* in April of 1999, and its subsequent publication in nine languages, our lives have become nothing short of nomadic. We've traveled worldwide with the model of nine choices, which has now become the foundation for everything we do—from keynote speaking on happiness and leadership, to executive team training in corporations, to medical research. Yet, even though we customize our programs to the needs of each group, we've been asked certain questions repeatedly. We think this is a fine opportunity to answer some of them, anticipating that you may have similar questions yourself.

What do you think about Prozac and other mood-altering pharmaceuticals?

Given that we are not trained medical professionals—and anyone using these drugs should be under the care of a professional!—we've observed that the mood-altering drugs seem to open up a window of opportunity for people. They feel less fatigued, depressed, debilitated, and thus able to live life more fully. The question is: Once you've found that open window, what choices will you make? And beyond the drugs, what behaviors will continue to keep you happiest? We believe that the nine happiness choices are a perfect companion to mood elevation. You feel better. Now it's time to make choices that lead to a happier and healthier life.

How can anyone be happy with all the misery in the world?

We, too, are often unhappy about the world's current political and social climate. But being personally unhappy has no positive effect on the world. In fact, unhappiness is draining and leaves us with little energy for the activist attitude and actions that would serve us well. If the world makes you unhappy, think again. You need the energy to make this a better place. Keep analyzing. Keep thinking, and, by all means, keep yourself happy. You'll be far more effective.

What is the relationship of happiness and money? Are happy people more successful?

Actually, yes, though the unit of measure isn't necessarily money. We've noted that happy people are more productive doing *anything* they choose to undertake. Sometimes this success leads them to money; other times it simply makes them the best practitioner in their chosen field, which might not be a money-oriented area. We've noticed in the dollar-focused corporate world that the most consistently successful people— those who thrive through the corporate hierarchy—are doing all the things on the happiness wheel. But, remember the age-old question: does money make you happy? As you might anticipate, our answer is a resounding NO. We'd reverse the equation and say: happiness will bring you abundance—in whatever profession or lifestyle you choose.

I'm working in an unhappy environment. What should I do?

If you have been entirely accountable and done everything you can to change this environment, to make it a happy place, we say "Run!" Change bosses, teams, divisions, corporations, and/or communities. We know that changing jobs is difficult and sometimes economically impossible. But, life is short. If you can make a change, do it. The emotional benefits and health outcomes of working in a low-stress, enjoyable atmosphere are well worth the trouble.

I feel guilty making myself happy. Shouldn't my children's needs come first?

This is a persistent question that comes to us mostly from young mothers. Parenting is an art requiring the accountable and exquisite balancing of your family's need with your own. It is something we each do differently. Our answer: Recognizing that you have extremely important responsibilities to your kids, you are ultimately hurting them if you don't take care of yourself. This means that, sometimes, you must put yourself first. Constantly putting the kids first is equivalent to putting your children's oxygen mask on first in an airplane emergency. You put yours on first so that you can be an effective parent. Harming yourself in favor of your children ultimately harms them too.

Every aspect of the happiness project has brought us great stimulation, growth and enjoyment in our public lives, but there is a personal story as well. As a result of countless hours spent in discussions of happiness, our own intentions to be happy have grown along with our awareness of all the other choices. We've become better parents, friends and lovers. We had a model of behavior that successfully carried us through our children's teen years, and is now a wonderful set of behaviors for continuing our relationships with the four kids we've nurtured into young adulthood. We can look carefully at the emotional content of all our relationships and see where they might be improved.

But the greatest gift of all remains the chance we had to get to know deeply happy people. With some, we have built friendships that we will treasure for the rest of our lives.

How about you? How do you get started?

The best way for most people to start is to select one choice on which to concentrate. You may want to revisit the Happiness Inventory in the introduction. If you scored low on one choice, you have the option to begin there. Sometimes just working with one choice will dramatically increase your overall level of happiness. From the starting point, you can systematically begin activating all the choices.

Choosing to be happy is a lifelong journey—a new way of life. As with all journeys, it will not always go as expected. Some days will feel more challenging than others. But now you have your guide. You know that happiness comes from within. You know that it takes an awareness of many choices, and, above all, it requires being true to yourself—a key to respecting who you really are. Happiness can be learned at any age, in any economic circumstances or geographical location, by people of any race, religion or belief system. You're ready. You have the tools. You have the insight. You have the power.

We wish you success on your adventure. And we wish you great happiness.

If you want to be happy, be.

Leo Tolstoy

Rick Foster (right) and Greg Hicks
Photograph of the authors by Steven Underhill

For information about our training programs and keynote
speeches please contact us at:

email: info@FosterHicks.com
phone: 510-540-6000

or visit us at our website www.choosetobehappy.com